CORTISOL DET COOKBOOK FOR WOMEN

Rebalance Your Hormones, Alleviate Stress, and Trim Your Waistline with Our 28-Day Meal Plan for a Total Wellness Transformation

Florence Smith

Copyright © 2024 by Florence Smith

All rights reserved. No part of this publication may be reproduced, distributed, or transmitted in any form or by any means, including photocopying, recording, or other electronic or mechanical methods, without the prior written permission of the publisher, except in the case of brief quotations embodied in critical reviews and certain other noncommercial uses permitted by copyright law.

TABLE OF CONTENTS

CHAPTER 1 11
The Power of Cortisol and the Path to a Stress-Free, Balanced Life 11
- How Stress Alters Hormones and Weight 12
- The Power of Food 14
- Why This Cookbook is Different 16

CHAPTER 2 19
The Hormonal Harmony Diet 19
- Top Superfoods for Cortisol Control and Hormonal Health 19
- Omega-3s: The Anti-Stress, Anti-Inflammatory Fat 21
- Adaptogens: Nature's Answer to Stress Management 23
- Fiber and Blood Sugar Balance 25
- The Truth About Sugar and Cortisol 27
- Why Your Gut Health Matters for Hormonal and Stress Balance 29

CHAPTER 3 31
100 Recipes 31
- Breakfast 31
- Cinnamon Almond Oatmeal 32
- Avocado & Spinach Smoothie 32
- Turmeric Coconut Porridge 33
- Chia Pudding with Berries 33
- Egg White & Veggie Scramble 34
- Almond Flour Pancakes 34
- Protein-Packed Smoothie 35
- Sweet Potato Hash with Poached Eggs 36

Flaxseed & Banana Muffins 36

Zucchini & Mushroom Frittata 37

Matcha & Almond Butter Smoothie 38

Overnight Oats with Walnuts and Berries 38

Coconut & Chia Seed Pudding 39

Avocado Toast with Lemon and Pumpkin Seeds 40

Apple Cinnamon Quinoa 40

Kefir & Berry Parfait 41

Nutritional Values (per serving): 41

Carrot Cake Oats 41

Coconut Milk Chia Pudding 42

Egg & Avocado Breakfast Wrap 43

Berry & Hemp Protein Smoothie 43

Cinnamon-Spiced Quinoa Porridge 44

Green Detox Smoothie 44

Pumpkin Spice Chia Pudding 45

Peanut Butter & Banana Oats 46

Mango Coconut Smoothie 46

Lunch 48

Quinoa & Chickpea Salad with Lemon Tahini Dressing 48

Grilled Chicken with Sweet Potato and Greens 49

Avocado, Cucumber, and Tomato Salad with Olive Oil Dressing 49

Turmeric Chicken Soup 50

Lentil & Kale Soup 51

Chia and Walnut Salad with Avocado and Lemon Vinaigrette 51

Salmon Salad with Spinach and Walnuts 52

Zucchini Noodles with Pesto & Grilled Chicken 53

Roasted Veggie & Hummus Wrap 53

Shrimp & Avocado Lettuce Wraps 54

Miso Soup with Tofu and Seaweed 54

Quinoa & Black Bean Buddha Bowl 55

Eggplant & Lentil Stew 56

Grilled Chicken Caesar Salad with Greek Yogurt Dressing 56

Salmon & Broccoli Stir-Fry 57

Cabbage & Carrot Slaw with Avocado 58

Grilled Veggie & Halloumi Salad 58

Sweet Potato & Black Bean Chili 59

Coconut & Lime Chicken with Mango Salad 60

Turkey & Avocado Lettuce Wraps 61

Spicy Quinoa & Vegetable Stir-Fry 61

Grilled Tofu with Spinach & Pine Nuts 62

Chickpea & Sweet Potato Buddha Bowl 63

Asian-Inspired Salmon Salad 64

Cauliflower Rice Stir-Fry with Vegetables 64

Dinner 66

Grilled Salmon with Roasted Brussels Sprouts and Quinoa 66

Turmeric and Ginger Chicken Stir-Fry 67

Spaghetti Squash with Pesto and Grilled Chicken 68

Lemon & Herb Baked Cod with Steamed Vegetables 68

Zucchini Noodles with Avocado Pesto 69

Grilled Chicken with Asparagus and Sweet Potato 70

Cauliflower & Chickpea Curry 71

Shrimp Stir-Fry with Bok Choy and Bell Peppers 72

Spaghetti Squash Primavera 72

Grilled Chicken with Mango Salsa and Brown Rice 73

Coconut-Lime Grilled Fish Tacos 74

Baked Salmon with Broccoli and Lemon 75

Spicy Turkey Meatballs with Cauliflower Rice 75

Miso-Glazed Salmon with Cucumber Salad 76

Eggplant & Lentil Stew with Garlic Bread 77

Garlic Butter Shrimp with Zoodles 78

Sweet Potato & Kale Buddha Bowl 79

Grilled Tempeh with Brussels Sprouts 80

Roasted Veggie & Quinoa Stir-Fry 80

Lemon Garlic Chicken with Sautéed Spinach 81

Salmon & Avocado Wraps 82

Grilled Steak with Roasted Vegetables 83

Sweet Potato & Black Bean Tacos 83

Lemon Herb Chicken with Roasted Sweet Potatoes 84

Teriyaki Salmon with Veggie Stir-Fry 85

Snacks 87

Avocado & Hummus Toast 87

Protein-Packed Energy Balls 87

Chia & Coconut Protein Bars 88

Baked Sweet Potato Fries 89

Greek Yogurt & Berry Parfait 90

Carrot Sticks with Almond Butter 90

Roasted Chickpeas with Turmeric 91

Apple with Almond Butter & Cinnamon 91

Celery & Peanut Butter Sticks 92

Coconut & Cashew Energy Bites 92

Spicy Roasted Pumpkin Seeds 93

Cucumber & Cream Cheese Bites 94

Roasted Veggie Chips 94

Almond & Date Protein Bars 95

Sweet Potato Chips with Guacamole 96

Edamame Beans with Sea Salt 97

Apple & Walnuts with Cinnamon 97

Zucchini Fries with Avocado Dip 98

Chia Seed Crackers 98

Cinnamon-Spiced Almonds 99

Coconut Yogurt with Berries 100

Grilled Veggie Skewers 101

Chocolate-Covered Almonds 101

Cucumber & Hummus Bites 102

Turmeric-Spiced Popcorn 103

CHAPTER 4 105

The 28-Day Meal Plan 105

28 day meal plan chart 105

Scan the QR Code and ACESS YOUR 3 EXCLUSIVE BONUSES NOW!!

🔥 Bonus 1: Hormonal Balance Shopping List

🔥 Bonus 2: Mindfulness and Relaxation Toolkit

🔥 Bonus 3: Cortisol-Reducing Herbal Remedies Guide

CHAPTER 1

The Power of Cortisol and the Path to a Stress-Free, Balanced Life

Known as the "stress hormone," cortisol is an essential body component. It manages our stress response, regulates metabolism, and controls the sleep-wake cycle. Its primary job is to increase alertness and boost energy in times of stress—a survival mechanism that served our ancestors when facing physical threats. However, chronic stress in today's society can lead to persistently elevated cortisol levels, which can have detrimental effects, especially on women's health.

For women, the effects of cortisol are particularly pronounced due to its impact on hormonal balance. Elevated cortisol can disrupt the delicate equilibrium of reproductive hormones, leading to irregular menstrual cycles, challenges with fertility, and exacerbated symptoms of menopause and perimenopause. These hormonal imbalances affect physical health and emotional well-being, contributing to mood swings and general discomfort.

Another significant impact of high cortisol levels is on body weight. Cortisol can increase appetite and signal the body to shift its metabolism towards storing fat rather than burning it. This often results in weight gain, particularly around the abdomen, which is linked to a higher risk of heart disease and diabetes. Managing cortisol levels is, therefore, crucial for maintaining a healthy weight and overall metabolic health.

Sleep is another area where cortisol plays a critical role. Typically, cortisol levels rise in the early morning to help wake us up and decline in the evening to allow our bodies to relax and prepare for sleep. However, when cortisol levels remain high at night, it can lead to difficulties falling asleep or staying asleep, resulting in less restorative sleep. This leaves one tired and less alert the next day and perpetuates the stress and cortisol production cycle.

The mental health implications of prolonged high cortisol are also significant. Chronic stress and high cortisol levels can lead to anxiety, depression, and irritability. These mood disorders can strain personal relationships and make daily tasks more challenging, further increasing stress and cortisol levels, thus continuing the cycle.

Moreover, an overtaxed cortisol system can weaken the immune system, making the body more susceptible to infections and slowing down recovery times from illness. This is particularly troubling for women, who may already be juggling multiple responsibilities that can contribute to stress levels.

Understanding the dual role of cortisol—as both a necessary hormone for survival and a potential health hazard when levels remain high—is crucial. For women, finding ways to manage stress and maintain cortisol balance is key to sustaining physical and emotional health. By incorporating stress-reduction techniques such as mindfulness, regular physical activity, and a balanced diet, women can help regulate their cortisol levels. This improves their overall health and enhances their quality of life, allowing them to engage more fully with the world around them without the burden of stress-induced health issues.

How Stress Alters Hormones and Weight

Stress, an all-too-familiar experience in modern life, significantly impacts our bodies, mainly through its intricate relationship with hormones and weight management. When we are under stress, our bodies release cortisol and other stress chemicals, which provide us with rapid energy and increased alertness. However, these biological responses can disrupt normal bodily functions in the long term, leading to a silent cycle of hormonal imbalance and weight gain.

Initially, the surge in cortisol provides the 'fight or flight' energy needed to deal with immediate challenges. This hormone also affects other vital hormones like adrenaline, which increases energy, and insulin, which regulates blood sugar levels. Usually, these hormonal fluctuations are temporary and stabilize as stress levels decrease. However, persistent stress prevents this return to balance, keeping cortisol levels elevated and disrupting the normal rhythm of hormone production.

Long-term elevated cortisol levels have serious consequences, particularly for women. One of the most noticeable impacts is insulin resistance. Cortisol helps regulate blood sugar by converting proteins and fats into glucose, a quick energy source. On the other hand, persistently elevated cortisol causes the body's cells to become less sensitive to insulin, which raises blood sugar levels and increases fat storage, especially around the middle. This fat is not merely aesthetic but metabolically active, releasing hormones and chemicals that can further disrupt hormonal balance.

The effects on appetite further complicate the relationship between stress, cortisol, and weight gain. Cortisol triggers cravings for high-fat, high-sugar foods that provide quick energy and pleasure, reinforcing the stress-eating cycle. This leads to weight gain and a more complex struggle to lose weight as the body clings to its fat reserves as a survival mechanism.

Moreover, chronic stress impacts reproductive hormones like estrogen and progesterone, which are crucial for regular menstrual cycles and overall reproductive health. The health landscape for women can be further complicated by imbalances in these hormones, which can result in a variety of problems, from irregular periods to more serious disorders like polycystic ovarian syndrome (PCOS).

The interplay between stress, cortisol, and weight forms a silent cycle, often unnoticed until significant health issues arise. This cycle can manifest through symptoms like fatigue, mood swings, and unexplained weight changes—signs that are sometimes dismissed or misattributed, delaying effective intervention.

Breaking this cycle requires a holistic approach. Stress-reduction methods like yoga, meditation, and deep breathing can lower cortisol levels. In addition to reducing stress, regular exercise also controls hormones and weight. Blood sugar can be stabilized, and the effects of cortisol on the body can be lessened with a balanced diet high in nutritious foods and low in processed carbohydrates and fats.

Understanding the silent cycle of how stress alters hormones and weight is crucial for taking control of one's health. By acknowledging the role of stress and its physiological impacts, women can take proactive steps towards maintaining hormonal balance and achieving a healthy weight, thus breaking the cycle and fostering overall wellness.

The Power of Food

Food profoundly impacts our bodies, influencing everything from our mood to our metabolism. For women struggling with the stress-hormone-weight cycle, the proper diet can serve as a powerful tool to restore balance and enhance well-being. Understanding how different foods interact with hormones and stress can enable women to make informed dietary choices that break this detrimental cycle and support overall health.

The relationship between diet and hormones is intricate. Foods heavy in unhealthy fats and refined sugars can worsen hormonal imbalances by raising insulin, blood sugar, and cortisol levels. This cortisol surge can result in weight gain, especially around the abdomen, which can further upset hormonal balance and provide serious health hazards. On the other hand, a diet high in whole, nutrient-dense meals can help control blood sugar levels, lessen oscillations in insulin and cortisol, and eventually help with weight management.

Omega-3 fatty acid-rich foods, such as salmon, flaxseeds, and walnuts, are crucial for lowering stress. These fats can help offset the adverse effects of elevated cortisol levels because of their well-known anti-inflammatory qualities. Additionally, omega-3s produce hormones that regulate mood and relaxation, naturally mitigating stress and promoting a sense of calm.

Whole grains, vegetables, and fruits high in fiber contain complex carbs that might assist in lowering blood sugar absorption. This lowers insulin and blood sugar spikes, which may increase cortisol production. These foods offer a consistent energy source that improves resilience to stress and mood stability.

Hormone synthesis and regulation depend on adequate protein intake. Foods like chicken, turkey, eggs, and legumes include amino acids, the building blocks of neurotransmitters like serotonin, which are crucial for mood control. Maintaining a balanced mood makes the temptation to turn to food for emotional comfort, aiding in weight management.

Antioxidants and phytonutrients found in vibrant fruits and vegetables fight oxidative stress, a cause of cortisol production and hormonal imbalance. Berries, leafy greens, and beets are among the foods that can shield cells from harm and promote hormonal balance.

Herbs like ashwagandha, rhodiola, and holy basil may help improve the body's resilience to stress and regulate cortisol levels. Incorporating these adaptogens into the diet can provide a natural method to enhance stress response and hormonal balance.

To leverage the power of food against the stress-hormone-weight cycle, it's essential to focus on regular, balanced meals and mindful eating. Skipping meals can lead to significant fluctuations in blood sugar and cortisol levels, worsening stress and hormonal imbalances. Instead, aim for a consistent eating schedule and include various key nutrients listed above in every meal.

Mindful eating practices also play a crucial role. Observing hunger signals and eating in a calm, comfortable environment may help the body absorb and process food more effectively. This enhances nutritional absorption and reduces digestive problems brought on by stress. This method helps achieve and maintain a healthy weight and promotes hormonal balance.

Moreover, hydration should be noticed. Sufficient water intake is crucial for all bodily functions, including hormone production and stress response. Feelings of hunger can often be mistaken for dehydration, so maintaining hydration can prevent unnecessary snacking and facilitate better weight management.

For women, particularly those dealing with the repercussions of hormonal imbalances and stress, adopting a diet focused on balance and nutrient density can be transformative. This dietary approach can stabilize hormones, reduce stress, and mitigate weight gain risks. It fosters not only physical health but also mental and emotional well-being, empowering women to handle life's challenges more effectively.

The power of food extends beyond simple nutrition—it's a foundational tool for combating the stress-hormone-weight cycle. By making strategic dietary choices, women can harness this power to reclaim control over their health, breaking the cycle of stress, hormonal imbalance, and unwanted weight gain. This proactive approach enhances immediate well-being and sets the stage for long-term health and vitality.

Why This Cookbook is Different

In a world teeming with diet books and health guides, the "Cortisol Detox Diet Cookbook for Women" stands out for its holistic approach to wellness. This cookbook explores the complex relationship between diet, stress, and hormonal health rather than just weight loss or calorie restriction, providing a holistic approach to nourishing the body, mind, and soul.

This cookbook recognizes that women's health issues, especially those related to cortisol and stress, cannot be addressed through dietary changes alone. It acknowledges the need for a supportive and sustainable lifestyle, encouraging hormonal balance and stress management. Each recipe and dietary recommendation within these pages is carefully crafted to positively influence cortisol levels, enhance mood, and promote overall hormonal health, ensuring that every meal brings you closer to holistic well-being.

The approach here is deeply rooted in the understanding that every aspect of our lives impacts our health. Stress, sleep, physical activity, and nutrition are all interlinked, each playing a crucial role in how we feel daily. For instance, the recipes in this book provide the nutrients needed to combat stress, balance hormones, and offer the energy necessary for physical activity, which is another key component of stress reduction and hormonal health.

Moreover, this cookbook emphasizes the importance of meal timing and composition, which can significantly affect how our bodies process food and manage stress. It includes guidelines for creating balanced meals that stabilize blood sugar levels, reduce inflammation, and manage the body's stress response. This is essential for preventing the spikes in cortisol that can lead to cravings and overeating.

Another aspect that makes this cookbook unique is its commitment to practical, realistic dietary changes. Recognizing that drastic dietary overhauls are challenging to maintain, the focus is on incremental, manageable modifications that can be sustained over the long term. This approach empowers women to make healthier choices without feeling overwhelmed, promoting lasting change beyond the kitchen.

The recipes themselves are designed with real life in mind. They are simple to prepare, require accessible ingredients, and cater to a busy lifestyle. Whether you are a seasoned cook or new to the kitchen, you'll find dishes that fit your skill level and time constraints, making incorporating healthy eating into your daily routine easier.

In addition to nourishing recipes, the book provides insights into other aspects of wellness, such as mindfulness and relaxation techniques. These are intended to complement the dietary advice, offering women tools to manage stress effectively and enhance their overall well-being.

Ultimately, "The Cortisol Detox Diet Cookbook for Women" is more than a cookbook. It is a guide to living well, designed to help women understand and manage the impact of cortisol on their health. By adopting the holistic practices found in this book, women can look forward to improved physical health and a greater sense of peace and well-being. This isn't just about making dietary changes; it's about transforming your life, one meal at a time.

CHAPTER 2

The Hormonal Harmony Diet

This section introduces a nutritional strategy focused on balancing hormones and combating stress. You'll learn about key foods and nutrients that help regulate cortisol, enhance mood, and support hormonal health. By incorporating these dietary choices, you can help stabilize your body's hormonal responses and reduce the impact of stress. Whether dealing with daily pressures or hormonal fluctuations due to menstrual cycles or menopause, the dietary practices outlined here offer a solid foundation for achieving excellent health and balance.

Top Superfoods for Cortisol Control and Hormonal Health

Managing cortisol and supporting hormonal health is crucial for overall well-being, and certain superfoods can play a significant role in this process. These nutrient-rich foods help regulate stress hormones and contribute to hormonal balance, making them valuable additions to any diet focused on health and wellness. Here's a closer look at some top superfoods that are particularly effective for cortisol control and hormonal health:

Avocados are a powerhouse of nutrients, featuring high levels of potassium, magnesium, and healthy fats. These help reduce blood pressure and cortisol levels. The fats in avocados are also essential for hormone production and can help regulate hormone levels.

Dark Chocolate contains flavonoids that have been shown to reduce cortisol levels. Consuming dark chocolate in moderation can also stimulate the production of endorphins, the body's natural mood elevators, which can alleviate stress.

Oily Fish such as salmon, mackerel, and sardines are rich in omega-3 fatty acids. These fats are known for their anti-inflammatory properties and ability to help reduce cortisol levels. Omega-3 fatty acids also regulate neurotransmitters, promote a balanced mood, and support brain health.

Leafy Greens like spinach, kale, and Swiss chard are high in magnesium, a mineral critical in controlling cortisol and managing stress. Magnesium also supports the biochemical reactions in the body that generate and use energy, which is vital for stress management.

Berries are another excellent food for hormonal health due to their high antioxidant content. Antioxidants help combat oxidative stress, which is linked to cortisol production. Blueberries, strawberries, and raspberries can help manage stress levels and reduce stress's physical and mental effects on the body.

Nuts and Seeds, such as almonds, flaxseeds, and chia seeds, are rich in omega-3 fatty acids, magnesium, and fiber. They help reduce inflammation and cortisol levels and provide essential nutrients for hormone production and regulation.

Citrus Fruits like oranges, lemons, and grapefruits are high in vitamin C, which has been shown to reduce cortisol levels and support the immune system. Vitamin C also helps produce progesterone, a hormone that can balance the effects of cortisol in the body.

Whole Grains such as oats, quinoa, and brown rice contain high B vitamins and magnesium levels, which help manage stress and cortisol levels. B vitamins are essential for the nervous system and can help the body rebound and recover from stress.

Legumes like lentils, chickpeas, and beans are not only rich in fiber, which helps slow the release of glucose into the blood, preventing sudden spikes in blood sugar and cortisol. They also contain bioactive compounds that support hormonal balance and stress reduction.

Yogurt and Other Fermented Foods such as kefir, sauerkraut, and kimchi are rich in probiotics, which promote a healthy gut. A well-functioning gut can profoundly impact overall health, including hormonal health and stress reduction, as it affects the production and regulation of key hormones like insulin, ghrelin, and leptin.

Including these superfoods in your diet can help manage cortisol levels and promote a more balanced hormonal profile. Each of these foods brings a unique set of nutrients that support the body's natural ability to regulate stress and maintain hormonal health. By integrating them into daily meals, you can create a diet that tastes good and provides significant health benefits. Whether you're experiencing stress due to everyday challenges or hormonal changes, these superfoods offer a natural way to enhance your body's resilience and promote long-term health and wellness.

Omega-3s: The Anti-Stress, Anti-Inflammatory Fat

Omega-3 fatty acids are often hailed as the cornerstone of a healthy diet, and they are noted for their extensive benefits, which range from enhancing brain function to reducing systemic inflammation. In terms of stress management and hormonal balance, omega-3s play a pivotal role, earning them the title of an anti-stress, anti-inflammatory powerhouse.

Omega-3 fatty acids, primarily found in fish like salmon, mackerel, and sardines, as well as in flaxseeds, chia seeds, and walnuts, are essential fats the body cannot produce on its own. This necessitates their inclusion through diet or supplements. The three main types of omega-3s are ALA (alpha-linolenic acid) found in plants, EPA (eicosapentaenoic acid), and DHA (docosahexaenoic acid), both predominantly found in marine sources. Each plays a unique role in bodily functions, with EPA and DHA particularly effective in managing bodily inflammation and neurological health.

One of the most significant impacts of omega-3s is their ability to modulate the body's response to stress. Stress activates the body's inflammatory pathways, and without adequate management, chronic inflammation can ensue, leading to a host of health issues, including accelerated aging and chronic diseases such as heart disease and arthritis. Omega-3 fatty acids help counteract this inflammation. Research suggests they can inhibit the production of molecules and substances linked to inflammation, such as inflammatory eicosanoids and cytokines.

In the realm of mental health, omega-3s are just as influential. They are vital components of cell membranes in the brain and are integral to cell receptor function. By improving cell receptor capabilities, omega-3s enhance neurotransmitter functions, including serotonin and dopamine, which play a key role in mood regulation. This is crucial for stress management, as adequate levels of these neurotransmitters can help prevent the mood swings associated with stress and depression.

Furthermore, omega-3 fatty acids have been found to reduce cortisol secretion during stressful episodes. Cortisol, the body's primary stress hormone, when secreted at high levels persistently, can lead to various health problems, including chronic stress and hormonal imbalances. Omega-3s help moderate the production and effect of cortisol, thereby supporting mental and physical health by maintaining a balanced hormonal environment.

For those dealing with high-stress levels, incorporating omega-3s into the diet can also aid in weight management and metabolic health. High cortisol levels can accumulate fat, particularly around the abdomen, and disrupt normal metabolic processes. By mitigating the impact of cortisol and helping to calm inflammation, omega-3s can help maintain a healthier metabolism, thus preventing the weight gain often associated with high stress.

The anti-inflammatory properties of omega-3s extend beyond managing stress. They are crucial in maintaining hormonal health overall, particularly in regulating hormones that affect the immune system and metabolism. Regular consumption of foods rich in omega-3s or quality supplements can help keep these hormonal processes within normal ranges, benefiting overall health.

Integrating omega-3s into the diet can be straightforward. For those who eat fish, incorporating servings of fatty fish several times a week can be highly beneficial. For vegetarians or those who prefer not to eat fish, options like flaxseeds, chia seeds, and walnuts are excellent sources of ALA, which the body can partially convert to EPA and DHA. Supplements, such as fish oil or algae oils, are also an effective way to ensure adequate intake of EPA and DHA.

The role of omega-3 fatty acids in managing stress and inflammation is well-documented and highly significant. Their incorporation into the daily diet can help mitigate the physical effects of stress, support mental health, and promote a balanced hormonal environment, leading to a healthier, more resilient body.

Adaptogens: Nature's Answer to Stress Management

Adaptogens are natural herbal remedies that enhance the body's resilience to stress. Originating from traditional Chinese and Ayurvedic medicine, these substances have been used for centuries to help the body adapt to various environmental and psychological stresses. Modern wellness practices celebrate adaptogens for their unique ability to regulate the adrenal system, which controls the hormonal stress response, promoting a more balanced internal environment.

The real power of adaptogens lies in their capacity to act as biological response modifiers. This means they can calm the body under stress and energize it when fatigued, essentially working to maintain equilibrium. This dual action makes adaptogens especially beneficial for those facing constant stress or those who need to sustain high levels of physical and mental stamina.

Among the most popular adaptogens are ashwagandha, which is known to reduce anxiety and stress while improving concentration; Rhodiola Rosea, which enhances mental performance and energy; ginseng, known for boosting energy and immune system strength; Holy Basil, or Tulsi, which helps normalize bodily processes affected by stress; and licorice root, which supports adrenal function and reduces fatigue. Each adaptogen has a unique set of benefits that contribute to stress reduction and overall vitality and health.

Adaptogens work by supporting the adrenal glands, helping the body manage and normalize cortisol levels—the primary stress hormone. This support helps mitigate the physical and psychological impacts of stress. Beyond alleviating stress, adaptogens possess anti-inflammatory and antioxidant properties, fight fatigue, and promote healthy aging. They enhance overall vitality, which in turn helps the body ward off chronic diseases and maintain optimal functioning.

Integrating adaptogens into one's diet can vary based on personal preference and the specific adaptogen's form. Many adaptogens, such as teas, powders, and supplements, allow for flexible incorporation into daily routines. For instance, ashwagandha and Rhodiola are often taken as supplements, while ginseng and Holy Basil can be brewed into teas. Starting with low doses is advisable to gauge how the body responds before gradually increasing the amount as needed.

However, consulting with a healthcare provider before beginning any new supplement is essential, particularly for those with existing health conditions or those taking other medications. Professional guidance ensures that adaptogens are used safely and effectively, tailored to individual health needs.

Adaptogens are a powerful tool for managing stress and enhancing overall health. By naturally balancing the body's stress response and supporting various bodily functions, adaptogens offer a holistic approach to maintaining health and wellness, making them valuable to any diet focused on achieving a balanced and healthy lifestyle.

Fiber and Blood Sugar Balance

Fiber plays a fundamental role in maintaining overall health, especially in regulating blood sugar levels. This, in turn, influences a broad range of bodily functions, including hormonal balance, appetite control, and metabolic health. Understanding the importance of fiber and its impact on blood sugar stability is essential for anyone looking to improve their dietary habits and overall wellness.

When you consume food, especially carbohydrates, your body breaks them down into glucose, which enters the bloodstream and raises your blood sugar levels. This increase triggers the pancreas to release insulin, a hormone that helps cells absorb and use glucose for energy. How quickly this process occurs and how dramatic the blood sugar spike is can depend significantly on the type of carbohydrates consumed—precisely, whether the food is high in fiber.

Fiber, found in plant foods like fruits, vegetables, whole grains, and legumes, is soluble and insoluble. Soluble fiber dissolves in water to form a gel-like substance in the gut, slowing down digestion. This slowdown allows for a more gradual absorption of glucose, leading to more moderate rises in blood sugar and insulin levels. On the other hand, insoluble fiber does not dissolve in water and helps add bulk to stool and move it through the digestive system, which can also help control blood sugar.

The benefits of a diet high in fiber extend beyond blood sugar control. By moderating the pace of digestion and the absorption of nutrients, fiber helps maintain a steady level of energy throughout the day. This stable energy helps curb the sudden hunger spikes and crashes that can lead to overeating and weight gain, thus supporting weight management and metabolic health.

Moreover, a steady blood sugar level helps prevent the development of insulin resistance, a condition in which cells become less sensitive to insulin and fail to absorb glucose efficiently. Insulin resistance is a precursor to more serious health issues, including type 2 diabetes and cardiovascular diseases. Fiber plays a preventative role in maintaining insulin sensitivity in these conditions.

In addition to metabolic health, the blood sugar stability facilitated by fiber intake also impacts hormonal balance. Fluctuations in blood sugar can cause fluctuations in other hormones, such as cortisol and adrenaline, the stress hormones. When blood sugar levels drop, the body perceives it as a stress signal and releases cortisol to increase sugar levels. This response raises blood sugar and can create a cycle of stress and hormonal imbalance that impacts overall health.

The impact of fiber on gut health also contributes significantly to its benefits. A healthy gut is crucial for overall health, affecting everything from the immune system to hormone production. Fiber serves as a prebiotic, feeding the good bacteria in the gut, which helps them thrive and maintain a healthy intestinal environment. These beneficial bacteria play a role in inflammation control, immune function, and even the production of certain hormones that regulate appetite and stress.

Consuming adequate amounts of fiber is not just about preventing diseases; it's about creating a foundation of good health. According to dietary guidelines, adults should aim for about 25 to 30 grams of fiber per day, yet many people fall short of this amount. To increase fiber intake, include a variety of fiber-rich foods in your diet, such as:

- **Whole grains**: Choose whole-grain bread, pasta, and cereals over refined grains.
- **Fruits and vegetables**: Eat a wide variety of colorful fruits and vegetables. Aim for at least five servings per day.
- **Legumes**: Incorporate beans, lentils, and other legumes into meals.

- **Nuts and seeds**: Snack on almonds, flaxseeds, or chia seeds, or add them to salads and yogurts.

Fiber's role in maintaining blood sugar balance is more significant than many might think. It not only helps manage immediate blood sugar and hormonal issues but also contributes to long-term health and disease prevention. By making fiber a focal point in your diet, you can enhance your health in a way that is simple, effective, and beneficial across many aspects of your well-being.

The Truth About Sugar and Cortisol

Sugar and cortisol share a complex, intertwined relationship that significantly impacts physical and emotional health. Understanding this dynamic is crucial for managing stress and maintaining overall wellness, especially in today's fast-paced, high-stress environment where sugary treats are often used as a quick fix for energy boosts.

Cortisol, known as the stress hormone, is released by the adrenal glands during physical and mental stress. Its primary role is to prepare the body to face immediate challenges by increasing glucose levels in the blood, enhancing the brain's use of glucose, and improving the availability of substances that repair tissues. However, cortisol increases appetite and cravings for sweet, fatty, or salty foods. This is where sugar comes into play, providing quick energy and temporary pleasure, which can seem relieving during stressful times.

The immediate effect of consuming sugar is a spike in blood sugar levels, providing a rush of energy and heightened alertness. The body responds to this sugar rush with a release of insulin to help absorb the excess glucose from the bloodstream, leading to a rapid drop in blood sugar levels, often referred to as a "crash." This crash can leave you feeling tired and irritable and craving more sugar to regain that energy high, thus creating a vicious cycle of sugar highs and lows.

This fluctuation in blood sugar levels forces the body to release more cortisol to stabilize the sugar levels, exacerbating the stress response and leading to a consistently elevated cortisol level in the blood. Over time, high cortisol levels can cause a plethora of health issues, including weight gain, immune dysfunction, and chronic diseases such as type 2 diabetes and heart disease. Furthermore, chronically high cortisol levels can affect cognitive functions, leading to impaired memory, decreased concentration, and an increased risk of depression.

The cycle of sugar intake and cortisol release does more than affect physical health; it also plays a significant role in emotional and mental well-being. The temporary mood boosts from sugar are indeed short-lived, and their aftermath can exacerbate feelings of anxiety and depression. Regular consumption of high-sugar foods can alter the brain's neurochemical balance, affecting neurotransmitters that regulate mood.

Reducing sugar intake can help break this cycle. Moderating sugar consumption can help stabilize blood sugar levels, which helps regulate cortisol levels and reduce the intensity of the body's stress response. More stable blood sugar levels can improve energy, a more balanced mood, and stress management capacity.

To manage sugar intake effectively, consider opting for whole foods that are low in added sugars and high in fiber, such as fruits, vegetables, and whole grains. These foods provide a slower, more consistent source of glucose for the body, which helps maintain stable blood sugar levels. Be mindful of hidden sugars in processed foods, which can be found in unexpected places like salad dressings, condiments, and breads. Also, replacing sugary snacks with healthier options and staying hydrated can help; sometimes, what feels like a sugar craving is dehydration.

The relationship between sugar and cortisol is a love-hate one. Sugar's immediate gratification comes at the cost of long-term health risks and increased stress levels. Understanding and managing this dynamic can improve your dietary habits and stress management techniques, leading to better health and a more balanced life.

Why Your Gut Health Matters for Hormonal and Stress Balance

The connection between gut health and overall well-being is increasingly recognized, particularly regarding its impact on hormonal balance and stress management. Often referred to as the "second brain," the gut boasts its extensive network of neurons and plays a vital role in regulating various bodily functions, including key hormone production and stress responses.

Numerous cells in the gastrointestinal tract produce and respond to hormones, influencing digestion, metabolism, and mood. For example, the gut creates a significant amount of the body's serotonin, which regulates mood, appetite, and sleep. When the gut's ability to make or process serotonin is disrupted, it can lead to mood disorders and impact overall emotional well-being.

The gut microbiome, which comprises a vast community of microorganisms in the intestinal tract, significantly influences the body's hormonal landscape. Some gut bacteria are involved in estrogen metabolism by producing an enzyme that helps convert estrogen into its active forms. An imbalance in these bacteria can lead to hormonal disruptions, such as mood swings and irregular menstrual cycles.

The gut's link to the body's stress response is also profound. The gut's enteric nervous system (ENS) communicates directly with the brain, influencing emotional and physiological responses. An imbalanced gut microbiome can disrupt this communication, leading to increased levels of stress and anxiety.

Moreover, a healthy gut helps regulate the release and normalization of cortisol, the stress hormone. During stress, the demand for cortisol rises, and a healthy gut can help modulate this response, preventing cortisol overproduction, which can be detrimental. High cortisol levels can suppress the immune system, increase blood pressure, and contribute to fatigue and mental cloudiness.

Chronic inflammation in the gut can lead to a "leaky gut," a condition where bacteria and toxins leak into the bloodstream, triggering an immune response and systemic inflammation. This can disrupt hormonal balance and exacerbate stress responses, perpetuating poor health.

Systemic inflammation from poor gut health can also affect the adrenal glands, pancreas, and thyroid, all crucial for hormone production and regulation. For example, inflammation can lead to insulin resistance, affecting blood sugar management, or disrupt thyroid function, impacting metabolism, energy levels, and mood.

To support gut health and, in turn, hormonal and stress balance, consider dietary and lifestyle changes that include increasing fiber intake, which promotes beneficial gut bacteria and a healthy gut barrier. Fiber-rich foods, such as vegetables, fruits, legumes, and whole grains, are helpful.

Incorporating probiotics and prebiotics can also be helpful. Probiotics introduce beneficial bacteria to the gut, while prebiotics provide the nutrients needed to nourish these bacteria. Foods like yogurt, kefir, sauerkraut, bananas, onions, and garlic are beneficial for gut health.

It is crucial to reduce the intake of inflammatory foods such as processed foods, sugars, and trans fats. Instead, focus on a diet rich in whole foods that provide antioxidants and natural anti-inflammatory compounds.

Managing stress is also essential, as chronic stress can directly impact gut health by altering gut bacteria and increasing gut permeability. Mindfulness, yoga, and regular exercise can help manage stress levels effectively.

Staying hydrated is essential for maintaining the mucosal lining of the intestines, which helps prevent a leaky gut.

CHAPTER 3

100 Recipes

Discover a collection of 100 delicious and nutritious recipes, each tailored to support hormonal balance and manage stress. The selection includes energizing breakfasts, nourishing lunches, satisfying dinners, and wholesome snacks. These recipes go beyond mere sustenance; they're designed with ingredients that help control cortisol levels and promote overall wellness. Whether you're a novice in the kitchen or an experienced cook, you'll find dishes here that cater to your taste buds while boosting your health, providing both inspiration and practical ways to enhance your dietary habits.

Breakfast

Start your day right with 25 breakfast recipes that do more than satisfy your morning hunger—they energize your body, stabilize your hormones, and help manage stress. Each dish is crafted with ingredients chosen for their health benefits, offering a perfect blend of flavor and nutrition. From smoothies packed with antioxidants to hearty oatmeals and protein-rich scrambles, these breakfasts are designed to kickstart your metabolism and keep you fueled throughout the morning. Enjoy exploring these varied options that cater to different tastes and dietary needs, setting a positive tone for the rest of your day.

Cinnamon Almond Oatmeal

- 1 cup rolled oats
- 2 cups almond milk
- 1 teaspoon ground cinnamon
- 2 tablespoons almond butter
- 1 tablespoon honey or maple syrup (optional)
- Pinch of salt
- Optional toppings: sliced almonds, fresh berries, a sprinkle of ground flaxseed

Directions:

1. In a medium saucepan, bring the almond milk to a low boil over medium heat. Add the oats and a pinch of salt, then reduce the heat to a simmer.
2. Stir in the ground cinnamon and almond butter, mixing thoroughly to combine all the ingredients.
3. Continue to cook the oats, stirring occasionally, until they have absorbed the almond milk and reached your desired consistency, typically about 5-7 minutes.
4. If you prefer a sweeter oatmeal, stir in honey or maple syrup to taste.
5. Serve the oatmeal hot, topped with sliced almonds, fresh berries, and a sprinkle of ground flaxseed for an extra boost of nutrients.

Nutritional Values (per serving):

- Calories: 315
- Fat: 14g
- Carbohydrates: 40g
- Protein: 9g

Avocado & Spinach Smoothie

Ingredients:

- 1 ripe avocado, peeled and pitted
- 1 cup fresh spinach leaves
- 1 banana
- 1/2 cup Greek yogurt
- 1 cup almond milk or water
- 1 tablespoon honey or maple syrup (optional)
- Ice cubes (optional)

Directions:

- In a blender, combine the avocado, spinach, banana, and Greek yogurt.
- Add the almond milk or water to facilitate blending. If you prefer a sweeter smoothie, add honey or maple syrup to taste.
- Blend on high until smooth and creamy. If the smoothie is too thick, add more almond milk or water until you reach the desired consistency.
- For a colder beverage, add a few ice cubes and blend again.
- Pour the smoothie into glasses and serve immediately for the freshest taste.

Nutritional Values (per serving):

- Calories: 240
- Fat: 15g
- Carbohydrates: 23g

- Protein: 6g

Turmeric Coconut Porridge

Ingredients:

- 1 cup rolled oats
- 1 can (about 14 oz) coconut milk
- 1 cup water
- 1 teaspoon ground turmeric
- 1/2 teaspoon cinnamon
- 1/4 teaspoon ground ginger
- Pinch of black pepper (to enhance turmeric absorption)
- 1 tablespoon honey or maple syrup (optional)
- Optional toppings: sliced bananas, shredded coconut, chopped nuts

Directions:

1. In a medium saucepan, combine the oats, coconut milk, and water. Bring the mixture to a boil over medium heat.
2. Reduce the heat to low and stir in the turmeric, cinnamon, ginger, and black pepper. Simmer, stirring occasionally, until the porridge has thickened and the oats are tender, about 5-7 minutes.
3. If a sweeter taste is desired, add honey or maple syrup and stir well.
4. Serve the porridge hot, garnished with optional toppings like sliced bananas, shredded coconut, and chopped nuts for added texture and flavor.

Nutritional Values (per serving):

- Calories: 310
- Fat: 18g
- Carbohydrates: 33g
- Protein: 6g

Chia Pudding with Berries

Ingredients:

- 1/4 cup chia seeds
- 1 cup almond milk or any other plant-based milk
- 1 tablespoon honey or maple syrup (optional)
- 1/2 teaspoon vanilla extract
- 1 cup mixed berries (such as strawberries, blueberries, and raspberries)

Directions:

1. In a mixing bowl, combine the chia seeds and almond milk. Stir well to ensure the seeds are evenly distributed.
2. Add the honey or maple syrup for sweetness and the vanilla extract for flavor. Mix thoroughly.
3. Cover the bowl with a lid or plastic wrap and refrigerate for at least 4 hours, preferably overnight. This allows the chia seeds to absorb the liquid and swell, forming a pudding-like consistency.
4. Before serving, give the pudding a good stir to break up any clumps. If the pudding is too thick, you can

add a little more milk to adjust the consistency.
5. Serve the chia pudding in bowls or glasses, topped with a generous helping of mixed berries.

Nutritional Values (per serving):

- Calories: 215
- Fat: 9g
- Carbohydrates: 30g
- Protein: 5g

Egg White & Veggie Scramble

Ingredients:

- 4 egg whites
- 1/2 cup chopped spinach
- 1/4 cup diced bell peppers (any color)
- 1/4 cup diced onions
- 1/4 cup chopped mushrooms
- 1 tablespoon olive oil
- Salt and pepper to taste
- Optional: shredded low-fat cheese, chopped herbs (such as parsley or chives)

Directions:

1. Heat the olive oil in a non-stick skillet over medium heat.
2. Add the diced onions and bell peppers to the skillet. Sauté for about 2-3 minutes until they start to soften.
3. Add the chopped mushrooms and cook for an additional 2 minutes until all the vegetables are tender.
4. Stir in the chopped spinach and cook until it wilts, about 1 minute.
5. In a bowl, whisk the egg whites with a pinch of salt and pepper until frothy.
6. Pour the egg whites over the sautéed vegetables in the skillet. Let them sit for about 1 minute without stirring to let the bottom set.
7. Gently stir the mixture, scrambling the eggs with the vegetables until the egg whites are fully cooked and no liquid remains, about 3-4 minutes.
8. If using, sprinkle shredded cheese and herbs over the scramble just before removing it from the heat. Allow the cheese to melt slightly.
9. Serve immediately while hot.

Nutritional Values (per serving):

- Calories: 180
- Fat: 8g
- Carbohydrates: 8g
- Protein: 18g

Almond Flour Pancakes

Ingredients:

- 1 cup almond flour
- 2 eggs
- 1/3 cup almond milk (or any milk of your choice)
- 1 tablespoon maple syrup or honey (optional for sweetness)
- 1 teaspoon vanilla extract
- 1/2 teaspoon baking powder

- Pinch of salt
- Coconut oil or butter for cooking
- Optional toppings: fresh berries, sliced bananas, a drizzle of honey or maple syrup

Directions:

1. In a mixing bowl, whisk together the almond flour, baking powder, and a pinch of salt.
2. In another bowl, beat the eggs and then mix in the almond milk, vanilla extract, and maple syrup or honey if using.
3. Pour the wet ingredients into the dry ingredients and stir until a smooth batter forms.
4. Heat a non-stick skillet over medium heat and lightly grease it with coconut oil or butter.
5. Pour small circles of batter onto the hot skillet (about 1/4 cup for each pancake). Cook for 2-3 minutes on one side until bubbles form on the surface and the edges begin to look set.
6. Flip the pancakes carefully and cook for another 2-3 minutes on the other side until golden and cooked through.
7. Remove from the skillet and repeat with the remaining batter, adding more oil or butter to the skillet as needed.
8. Serve the pancakes hot with your choice of toppings like fresh berries, sliced bananas, or a drizzle of honey or maple syrup.

Nutritional Values (per serving):

- Calories: 275
- Fat: 23g
- Carbohydrates: 12g
- Protein: 11g

Protein-Packed Smoothie

Ingredients:

- 1 scoop of your favorite protein powder (vanilla or unflavored works well)
- 1 cup unsweetened almond milk
- 1/2 banana
- 1/4 cup Greek yogurt
- 1 tablespoon natural peanut butter or almond butter
- 1 tablespoon flaxseeds
- Ice cubes (optional, for a thicker smoothie)

Directions:

1. Place all ingredients in a blender, starting with the almond milk to facilitate easier blending.
2. Add the banana, Greek yogurt, peanut butter, flaxseeds, and protein powder. If you prefer a colder, thicker smoothie, add a handful of ice cubes.
3. Blend on high until smooth and creamy. Ensure all components are thoroughly mixed and the smoothie has reached your desired consistency.

4. Pour into a glass and serve immediately for the freshest flavor and best texture.

Nutritional Values (per serving):

- Calories: 330
- Fat: 14g
- Carbohydrates: 27g
- Protein: 25g

Sweet Potato Hash with Poached Eggs

Ingredients:

- 2 medium sweet potatoes, peeled and diced
- 1 red bell pepper, diced
- 1 medium onion, diced
- 2 cloves garlic, minced
- 4 eggs
- 2 tablespoons olive oil
- Salt and pepper to taste
- Optional: fresh herbs such as parsley or chives for garnish

Directions:

1. Heat olive oil in a large skillet over medium heat. Add the diced sweet potatoes and cook, stirring occasionally, until they start to soften, about 5-7 minutes.
2. Add the diced onion and red bell pepper to the skillet. Cook for an additional 5 minutes, or until the vegetables are tender and the sweet potatoes are golden and crispy.
3. Stir in the minced garlic and cook for another minute until fragrant. Season the hash with salt and pepper to taste.
4. While the hash cooks, bring a pot of water to a gentle simmer. Add a small splash of vinegar. Crack each egg into a separate small bowl and gently slide them into the simmering water one at a time. Poach the eggs for about 3-4 minutes for soft yolks or longer if you prefer firmer yolks.
5. Use a slotted spoon to remove the poached eggs from the water and drain them on a paper towel.
6. To serve, divide the sweet potato hash among plates and top each serving with a poached egg. Garnish with chopped fresh herbs if using.

Nutritional Values (per serving):

- Calories: 320
- Fat: 18g
- Carbohydrates: 28g
- Protein: 12g

Flaxseed & Banana Muffins

Ingredients:

- 1 1/2 cups whole wheat flour
- 1/2 cup ground flaxseed
- 1 teaspoon baking powder
- 1/2 teaspoon baking soda
- 1/4 teaspoon salt
- 1 teaspoon cinnamon
- 3 ripe bananas, mashed
- 1/3 cup unsweetened applesauce
- 1/4 cup honey or maple syrup

- 1 egg
- 1 teaspoon vanilla extract
- Optional: 1/2 cup chopped nuts or dark chocolate chips for added texture

Directions:

- Preheat your oven to 350°F (175°C) and line a muffin tin with paper liners or grease it with a little oil.
- In a large bowl, combine the whole wheat flour, ground flaxseed, baking powder, baking soda, salt, and cinnamon.
- In another bowl, mix the mashed bananas, unsweetened applesauce, honey or maple syrup, egg, and vanilla extract until well combined.
- Pour the wet ingredients into the dry ingredients and stir until just combined. Avoid overmixing to keep the muffins light and fluffy.
- If using, fold in the chopped nuts or chocolate chips.
- Divide the batter evenly among the muffin cups, filling each about three-quarters full.
- Bake in the preheated oven for 18-20 minutes, or until a toothpick inserted into the center of a muffin comes out clean.
- Allow the muffins to cool in the pan for a few minutes before transferring them to a wire rack to cool completely.

Nutritional Values (per serving):

- Calories: 190
- Fat: 6g
- Carbohydrates: 32g
- Protein: 5g

Zucchini & Mushroom Frittata

Ingredients:

- 6 eggs
- 1 medium zucchini, thinly sliced
- 1 cup sliced mushrooms
- 1 small onion, finely chopped
- 2 cloves garlic, minced
- 1/2 cup grated Parmesan cheese
- 2 tablespoons olive oil
- Salt and pepper to taste
- Optional: chopped fresh herbs such as parsley or basil for garnish

Directions:

- Preheat your oven to 375°F (190°C).
- Heat olive oil in a 10-inch oven-safe skillet over medium heat. Add the onion and garlic, and sauté until the onion becomes translucent, about 3-4 minutes.
- Add the sliced mushrooms and zucchini to the skillet. Cook, stirring occasionally, until the vegetables are tender and lightly browned, about 5-7 minutes.
- In a large bowl, beat the eggs with salt, pepper, and half of the grated Parmesan. Pour this mixture over the cooked vegetables in the

- skillet, making sure the eggs cover all the vegetables evenly.
- Cook on the stovetop over medium heat until the edges of the frittata start to set but the center is still slightly runny, about 2-3 minutes.
- Sprinkle the remaining Parmesan cheese over the top of the frittata.
- Transfer the skillet to the preheated oven and bake until the frittata is set and golden on top, about 10-15 minutes.
- Remove from the oven and let it cool slightly before slicing. Garnish with fresh herbs if using.
- Serve warm or at room temperature.

Nutritional Values (per serving):

- Calories: 210
- Fat: 15g
- Carbohydrates: 5g
- Protein: 14g

Matcha & Almond Butter Smoothie

Ingredients:

- 1 teaspoon matcha green tea powder
- 1 banana
- 1 tablespoon almond butter
- 1 cup unsweetened almond milk
- 1/2 cup Greek yogurt (optional for added protein and creaminess)
- 1 tablespoon honey or agave syrup (optional for sweetness)
- Ice cubes (optional for a thicker, colder smoothie)

Directions:

1. Place the banana, almond butter, matcha green tea powder, and almond milk in a blender.
2. Add Greek yogurt for a creamier texture and extra protein, if desired.
3. If a sweeter taste is preferred, include honey or agave syrup.
4. Add a handful of ice cubes if you like your smoothies cold and thick.
5. Blend on high until all ingredients are thoroughly combined and the smoothie has reached a smooth, creamy consistency.
6. Taste and adjust sweetness or thickness by adding more honey or ice if needed, then blend again briefly.
7. Pour the smoothie into a glass and serve immediately for the best flavor and nutrient retention.

Nutritional Values (per serving):

- Calories: 280
- Fat: 12g
- Carbohydrates: 36g
- Protein: 10g

Overnight Oats with Walnuts and Berries

Ingredients:

- 1/2 cup rolled oats

- 1/2 cup unsweetened almond milk or any milk of your choice
- 1/2 cup Greek yogurt
- 1 tablespoon chia seeds
- 1 tablespoon honey or maple syrup (optional for sweetness)
- 1/4 cup walnuts, chopped
- 1/2 cup mixed berries (such as blueberries, raspberries, and blackberries)
- Optional: a sprinkle of cinnamon or vanilla extract for extra flavor

Directions:

1. In a mason jar or a sealable container, combine the rolled oats, almond milk, Greek yogurt, and chia seeds.
2. Add honey or maple syrup if you prefer your oats a bit sweeter. Stir in cinnamon or vanilla extract if using.
3. Mix all the ingredients together until well combined.
4. Top with chopped walnuts and a generous layer of mixed berries.
5. Seal the jar or container and refrigerate overnight, or for at least 6 hours.
6. In the morning, give the oats a good stir to mix in the flavors from the berries and nuts that may have settled on top.
7. Serve chilled, straight from the fridge.

Nutritional Values (per serving):

- Calories: 345
- Fat: 15g
- Carbohydrates: 45g
- Protein: 12g

Coconut & Chia Seed Pudding

Ingredients:

- 1/4 cup chia seeds
- 1 cup coconut milk (preferably full-fat for creaminess)
- 1 tablespoon honey or maple syrup (optional, for sweetness)
- 1/2 teaspoon vanilla extract
- Optional toppings: fresh mango cubes, pineapple chunks, or shredded coconut

Directions:

1. In a mixing bowl, combine the chia seeds and coconut milk. Stir well to ensure the seeds are evenly distributed.
2. Add the vanilla extract and honey or maple syrup, if using, to sweeten the pudding.
3. Mix all the ingredients thoroughly. Make sure the chia seeds are fully immersed in the coconut milk to avoid clumps.
4. Cover the bowl with a lid or plastic wrap and refrigerate for at least 4 hours, or overnight, allowing the chia seeds to absorb the coconut milk and swell up, creating a pudding-like consistency.

5. Once set, give the pudding a good stir to ensure the texture is even and creamy. Adjust the sweetness if necessary by adding a bit more honey or syrup.
6. Serve the pudding in bowls or glasses, topped with your choice of fresh mango cubes, pineapple chunks, or a sprinkle of shredded coconut for added flavor and texture.

Nutritional Values (per serving):

- Calories: 280
- Fat: 22g
- Carbohydrates: 20g
- Protein: 5g

Avocado Toast with Lemon and Pumpkin Seeds

Ingredients:

- 2 slices of whole-grain bread
- 1 ripe avocado
- 1 teaspoon fresh lemon juice
- 2 tablespoons pumpkin seeds
- Salt and pepper to taste
- Optional toppings: red pepper flakes, microgreens, or a drizzle of olive oil

Directions:

1. Toast the whole-grain bread slices until golden and crisp.
2. While the bread is toasting, halve the avocado and remove the pit. Scoop the avocado flesh into a bowl and mash it with a fork until creamy.
3. Stir in the fresh lemon juice and season with salt and pepper to taste.
4. Spread the mashed avocado evenly onto the toasted bread slices.
5. Sprinkle the pumpkin seeds generously over the avocado.
6. Add optional toppings, such as a pinch of red pepper flakes for heat, microgreens for freshness, or a light drizzle of olive oil for extra richness.
7. Serve immediately while the toast is still warm and crisp.

Nutritional Values (per serving):

- Calories: 260
- Fat: 18g
- Carbohydrates: 18g
- Protein: 6g

Apple Cinnamon Quinoa

Ingredients:

- 1/2 cup quinoa, rinsed
- 1 cup unsweetened almond milk or water
- 1 medium apple, diced
- 1 teaspoon ground cinnamon
- 1 tablespoon honey or maple syrup (optional for sweetness)
- 1/4 teaspoon vanilla extract
- Optional toppings: chopped walnuts, raisins, or a sprinkle of ground flaxseed

Directions:

1. In a medium saucepan, combine the rinsed quinoa and almond milk (or water). Bring to a boil over medium heat.
2. Reduce the heat to low, cover the saucepan, and let the quinoa simmer for about 10-12 minutes, or until most of the liquid is absorbed.
3. Stir in the diced apple, cinnamon, honey or maple syrup (if using), and vanilla extract. Continue cooking for another 5 minutes, stirring occasionally, until the apple softens and the quinoa is tender.
4. Remove the saucepan from the heat and let the quinoa sit, covered, for a couple of minutes to absorb any remaining liquid.
5. Serve the quinoa warm, topped with optional additions like chopped walnuts, raisins, or a sprinkle of ground flaxseed for added flavor and nutrition.

Nutritional Values (per serving):

- Calories: 230
- Fat: 4g
- Carbohydrates: 42g
- Protein: 6g

Kefir & Berry Parfait

Ingredients:

- 1 cup plain kefir
- 1/2 cup mixed fresh berries (such as strawberries, blueberries, and raspberries)
- 1/4 cup granola or crushed nuts
- 1 teaspoon honey or maple syrup (optional for sweetness)
- Optional toppings: a sprinkle of chia seeds or shredded coconut

Directions:

1. In a glass or small bowl, pour 1/3 of the kefir as the base layer.
2. Add a layer of mixed fresh berries on top of the kefir.
3. Sprinkle a layer of granola or crushed nuts over the berries for added texture and crunch.
4. Repeat the layering process with the remaining kefir, berries, and granola until the glass is full.
5. If desired, drizzle a small amount of honey or maple syrup over the top layer for sweetness.
6. Garnish with optional toppings like chia seeds or shredded coconut for an extra nutritional boost.
7. Serve immediately and enjoy.

Nutritional Values (per serving):

- Calories: 220
- Fat: 7g
- Carbohydrates: 29g
- Protein: 9g

Carrot Cake Oats

Ingredients:

- 1/2 cup rolled oats

- 1 cup unsweetened almond milk or water
- 1/2 cup grated carrot
- 1/2 teaspoon ground cinnamon
- 1/4 teaspoon ground nutmeg
- 1 tablespoon maple syrup or honey (optional for sweetness)
- 1 tablespoon chopped walnuts or pecans
- 1 tablespoon raisins (optional)
- 1 teaspoon vanilla extract
- Optional toppings: shredded coconut, Greek yogurt, or extra chopped nuts

Directions:

1. In a medium saucepan, combine the rolled oats, almond milk, grated carrot, cinnamon, nutmeg, and a pinch of salt. Stir to mix evenly.
2. Place the saucepan over medium heat and bring the mixture to a gentle simmer. Stir occasionally to prevent sticking.
3. Cook for about 5-7 minutes, or until the oats are tender and the mixture has thickened.
4. Stir in the maple syrup or honey, vanilla extract, and raisins if using. Mix well to incorporate all the flavors.
5. Remove from heat and transfer the oats to a bowl.
6. Top with chopped walnuts or pecans, and optional toppings like shredded coconut or a dollop of Greek yogurt for added texture and flavor.
7. Serve warm and enjoy.

Nutritional Values (per serving):

- Calories: 280
- Fat: 10g
- Carbohydrates: 40g
- Protein: 7g

Coconut Milk Chia Pudding

Ingredients:

- 1/4 cup chia seeds
- 1 cup coconut milk (full-fat for creaminess or light for a lower calorie option)
- 1 tablespoon honey or maple syrup (optional, for sweetness)
- 1/2 teaspoon vanilla extract
- Optional toppings: fresh berries, sliced mango, shredded coconut, or chopped nuts

Directions:

1. In a medium mixing bowl, combine the chia seeds and coconut milk. Stir well to ensure the seeds are evenly distributed and fully immersed in the liquid.
2. Add the honey or maple syrup and vanilla extract, stirring to incorporate the flavors.
3. Cover the bowl with a lid or plastic wrap and refrigerate for at least 4 hours, or overnight, allowing the chia seeds to absorb the coconut

milk and create a thick, pudding-like consistency.
4. Once set, stir the pudding to break up any clumps and ensure an even texture. Adjust the sweetness if desired by adding a bit more honey or syrup.
5. Serve the pudding in bowls or glasses, topped with your choice of fresh berries, mango slices, shredded coconut, or chopped nuts for added texture and flavor.

Nutritional Values (per serving):

- Calories: 250
- Fat: 18g
- Carbohydrates: 18g
- Protein: 5g

Egg & Avocado Breakfast Wrap

Ingredients:

- 1 large whole-grain tortilla
- 2 eggs
- 1/2 ripe avocado
- 1/4 cup baby spinach leaves
- 2 tablespoons shredded cheese (optional)
- Salt and pepper to taste
- 1 teaspoon olive oil or butter

Directions:

1. Heat a non-stick skillet over medium heat and add the olive oil or butter.
2. Crack the eggs into the skillet and scramble them gently, cooking until just set. Season with salt and pepper to taste. Remove from heat.
3. Mash the avocado in a small bowl and season lightly with salt and pepper.
4. Warm the tortilla in a dry skillet for about 30 seconds on each side or until soft and pliable.
5. Spread the mashed avocado evenly across the tortilla.
6. Layer the scrambled eggs on top of the avocado, followed by the baby spinach leaves. If using shredded cheese, sprinkle it over the top.
7. Roll the tortilla tightly into a wrap, tucking in the edges as you go.
8. Slice in half if desired and serve immediately.

Nutritional Values (per serving):

- Calories: 350
- Fat: 20g
- Carbohydrates: 28g
- Protein: 15g

Berry & Hemp Protein Smoothie

Ingredients:

- 1 cup mixed berries (such as blueberries, raspberries, and strawberries)
- 1 cup unsweetened almond milk or water
- 1 scoop hemp protein powder
- 1/2 banana
- 1 tablespoon chia seeds
- 1 teaspoon honey or maple syrup (optional, for sweetness)

- Ice cubes (optional, for a thicker smoothie)

Directions:

1. In a blender, combine the mixed berries, almond milk, hemp protein powder, banana, and chia seeds.
2. If you prefer a sweeter taste, add honey or maple syrup. For a colder and thicker consistency, add a handful of ice cubes.
3. Blend on high until smooth and creamy, ensuring all the ingredients are well incorporated.
4. Pour the smoothie into a glass and serve immediately for the freshest flavor and best texture.

Nutritional Values (per serving):

- Calories: 230
- Fat: 6g
- Carbohydrates: 33g
- Protein: 12g

Cinnamon-Spiced Quinoa Porridge

Ingredients:

- 1/2 cup quinoa, rinsed
- 1 cup unsweetened almond milk or water
- 1 teaspoon ground cinnamon
- 1/4 teaspoon ground nutmeg
- 1 tablespoon honey or maple syrup (optional, for sweetness)
- 1/2 teaspoon vanilla extract
- Optional toppings: sliced banana, chopped walnuts, raisins, or a sprinkle of ground flaxseed

Directions:

1. In a medium saucepan, combine the rinsed quinoa, almond milk, cinnamon, and nutmeg. Stir to mix evenly.
2. Bring the mixture to a boil over medium heat, then reduce the heat to low and cover the saucepan. Simmer for about 10-12 minutes, or until the quinoa has absorbed most of the liquid and is tender.
3. Stir in the honey or maple syrup (if using) and the vanilla extract. Cook for another 2-3 minutes to combine the flavors and achieve a creamy consistency.
4. Remove from heat and let the porridge sit for a minute or two. If the porridge is too thick, you can add a splash of almond milk to adjust the consistency.
5. Serve the quinoa porridge warm, topped with your choice of sliced banana, chopped walnuts, raisins, or ground flaxseed for added texture and nutrition.

Nutritional Values (per serving):

- Calories: 240
- Fat: 5g
- Carbohydrates: 40g
- Protein: 8g

Green Detox Smoothie

Ingredients:

- 1 cup fresh spinach leaves
- 1/2 cucumber, peeled and chopped

- 1 green apple, cored and sliced
- 1/2 avocado
- 1 tablespoon fresh lemon juice
- 1 cup unsweetened coconut water or water
- 1 teaspoon grated ginger (optional, for added detox benefits)
- Ice cubes (optional, for a colder smoothie)

Directions:

1. In a blender, combine the spinach, cucumber, green apple, avocado, lemon juice, and coconut water.
2. Add the grated ginger if you like a bit of a zing and extra detoxifying properties.
3. Blend on high until the mixture is smooth and creamy. If you prefer a colder, thicker smoothie, add a handful of ice cubes and blend again.
4. Taste the smoothie and adjust the flavor by adding a bit more lemon juice if needed.
5. Pour into a glass and serve immediately for the best flavor and nutrient retention.

Nutritional Values (per serving):

- Calories: 190
- Fat: 10g
- Carbohydrates: 24g
- Protein: 3g

Pumpkin Spice Chia Pudding

Ingredients:

- 1/4 cup chia seeds
- 1 cup unsweetened almond milk or coconut milk
- 1/4 cup pumpkin puree (not pumpkin pie filling)
- 1 tablespoon maple syrup or honey (optional, for sweetness)
- 1/2 teaspoon pumpkin pie spice
- 1/4 teaspoon vanilla extract
- Optional toppings: chopped pecans, shredded coconut, or a sprinkle of cinnamon

Directions:

1. In a medium mixing bowl, whisk together the almond milk, pumpkin puree, maple syrup or honey (if using), pumpkin pie spice, and vanilla extract until smooth.
2. Stir in the chia seeds, ensuring they are evenly distributed in the mixture to avoid clumping.
3. Cover the bowl with a lid or plastic wrap and refrigerate for at least 4 hours, or preferably overnight, to allow the chia seeds to absorb the liquid and create a pudding-like texture.
4. Once set, stir the pudding thoroughly to ensure an even consistency. If the pudding is too thick, add a splash of almond milk to adjust.

5. Serve the pudding in bowls or glasses, topped with your choice of pecans, shredded coconut, or a sprinkle of cinnamon for added flavor and texture.

Nutritional Values (per serving):

- Calories: 230
- Fat: 12g
- Carbohydrates: 22g
- Protein: 6g

Peanut Butter & Banana Oats

Ingredients:

- 1/2 cup rolled oats
- 1 cup unsweetened almond milk or water
- 1 ripe banana, sliced
- 1 tablespoon natural peanut butter
- 1/2 teaspoon cinnamon
- Optional toppings: chopped peanuts, a drizzle of honey, or a sprinkle of chia seeds

Directions:

1. In a medium saucepan, combine the rolled oats and almond milk. Cook over medium heat, stirring occasionally, until the oats have absorbed most of the liquid and are tender, about 5-7 minutes.
2. Stir in the cinnamon and half of the banana slices, mashing the banana slightly into the oats for added sweetness and creaminess.
3. Remove from heat and transfer the oatmeal to a serving bowl.
4. Dollop the peanut butter on top and gently swirl it into the oats. Arrange the remaining banana slices on top for presentation.
5. Add optional toppings like chopped peanuts, a drizzle of honey, or a sprinkle of chia seeds for extra texture and flavor.
6. Serve warm and enjoy.

Nutritional Values (per serving):

- Calories: 310
- Fat: 12g
- Carbohydrates: 45g
- Protein: 9g

Mango Coconut Smoothie

Ingredients:

- 1 cup fresh or frozen mango chunks
- 1/2 cup coconut milk (full-fat for creaminess or light for fewer calories)
- 1/2 cup unsweetened coconut water or water
- 1/2 banana
- 1 teaspoon honey or maple syrup (optional, for sweetness)
- Ice cubes (optional, for a thicker smoothie)
- Optional toppings: shredded coconut or chia seeds

Directions:

1. In a blender, combine the mango chunks, coconut milk, coconut water, and banana.

2. Add honey or maple syrup if you prefer a sweeter taste. For a colder, thicker texture, include a handful of ice cubes.
3. Blend on high until smooth and creamy, ensuring all the ingredients are fully combined.
4. Taste and adjust sweetness if needed, blending again briefly.
5. Pour into a glass and garnish with optional toppings like shredded coconut or chia seeds for an extra tropical flair.
6. Serve immediately while cold and fresh.

Nutritional Values (per serving):

- Calories: 210
- Fat: 10g
- Carbohydrates: 30g
- Protein: 2g

Lunch

Lunchtime is an opportunity to refuel your body with nourishing and satisfying meals that keep your energy levels steady throughout the day. In this section, you'll find 25 balanced and flavorful recipes designed to support hormonal health, manage stress, and promote overall wellness. Each dish combines wholesome ingredients with vibrant flavors, offering options that are as easy to prepare as they are enjoyable to eat. From hearty salads and protein-packed bowls to comforting soups and wraps, these recipes cater to a variety of tastes and dietary preferences, helping you stay nourished and energized.

Quinoa & Chickpea Salad with Lemon Tahini Dressing

Ingredients:

- 1 cup cooked quinoa
- 1 cup canned chickpeas, rinsed and drained
- 1/2 cup cherry tomatoes, halved
- 1/2 cup cucumber, diced
- 1/4 cup red onion, finely chopped
- 2 tablespoons fresh parsley, chopped
- 2 tablespoons fresh mint, chopped (optional)
- For the Lemon Tahini Dressing:
- 2 tablespoons tahini
- 2 tablespoons fresh lemon juice
- 1 tablespoon olive oil
- 1 teaspoon honey or maple syrup (optional, for sweetness)
- 1 clove garlic, minced
- 2-3 tablespoons water (to thin the dressing)
- Salt and pepper to taste

Directions:

1. In a large mixing bowl, combine the cooked quinoa, chickpeas, cherry tomatoes, cucumber, red onion, parsley, and mint if using.
2. In a small bowl, whisk together the tahini, lemon juice, olive oil, honey or maple syrup (if using), minced garlic, salt, and pepper. Add water gradually, whisking until the dressing reaches your desired consistency.
3. Pour the dressing over the quinoa and chickpea mixture. Toss everything together until well coated.
4. Taste and adjust seasonings as needed, adding more lemon juice, salt, or pepper to suit your preference.
5. Serve immediately or refrigerate for 15-20 minutes to allow the flavors to meld together.

Nutritional Values (per serving):

- Calories: 290
- Fat: 12g
- Carbohydrates: 38g
- Protein: 9g

Grilled Chicken with Sweet Potato and Greens

Ingredients:

- 1 medium sweet potato, peeled and cut into cubes
- 1 boneless, skinless chicken breast
- 2 cups mixed greens (such as spinach, arugula, or kale)
- 1 tablespoon olive oil
- 1 teaspoon paprika
- 1/2 teaspoon garlic powder
- Salt and pepper to taste
- Optional: balsamic glaze or lemon wedges for serving

Directions:

1. Preheat your oven to 400°F (200°C). Toss the sweet potato cubes with 1/2 tablespoon of olive oil, paprika, garlic powder, salt, and pepper. Spread them evenly on a baking sheet and roast for 20-25 minutes, turning halfway through, until tender and slightly crispy.
2. While the sweet potatoes are roasting, season the chicken breast with salt, pepper, and a drizzle of olive oil. Heat a grill pan or outdoor grill over medium-high heat.
3. Grill the chicken for 6-7 minutes per side, or until fully cooked and the internal temperature reaches 165°F (75°C). Remove the chicken from the grill and let it rest for 5 minutes before slicing.
4. Arrange the mixed greens on a plate or in a shallow bowl. Top with the roasted sweet potatoes and sliced grilled chicken.
5. If desired, drizzle with balsamic glaze or serve with a wedge of lemon for added flavor.

Nutritional Values (per serving):

- Calories: 340
- Fat: 9g
- Carbohydrates: 28g
- Protein: 35g

Avocado, Cucumber, and Tomato Salad with Olive Oil Dressing

Ingredients:

- 1 ripe avocado, diced
- 1 cup cucumber, diced
- 1 cup cherry tomatoes, halved
- 1/4 cup red onion, thinly sliced
- 2 tablespoons fresh parsley or basil, chopped
- 2 tablespoons olive oil
- 1 tablespoon fresh lemon juice
- Salt and pepper to taste

Directions:

1. In a large mixing bowl, combine the diced avocado, cucumber,

cherry tomatoes, red onion, and parsley or basil.
2. In a small bowl, whisk together the olive oil, lemon juice, salt, and pepper until well combined.
3. Drizzle the dressing over the salad and gently toss to coat all the ingredients evenly, taking care not to mash the avocado.
4. Taste and adjust the seasoning as needed, adding more lemon juice or salt if desired.
5. Serve immediately as a light and refreshing lunch or side dish.

Nutritional Values (per serving):

- Calories: 250
- Fat: 20g
- Carbohydrates: 16g
- Protein: 3g

Turmeric Chicken Soup

Ingredients:

- 1 tablespoon olive oil
- 1 medium onion, diced
- 2 cloves garlic, minced
- 1 teaspoon ground turmeric
- 1/2 teaspoon ground ginger
- 1/2 teaspoon cumin
- 2 medium carrots, sliced
- 1 celery stalk, diced
- 1 cup cooked shredded chicken (rotisserie chicken works well)
- 4 cups low-sodium chicken broth
- 1/2 cup coconut milk (optional, for creaminess)
- 1 cup spinach or kale leaves
- Juice of 1/2 lemon
- Salt and pepper to taste

Directions:

1. Heat the olive oil in a large pot over medium heat. Add the diced onion and garlic, and sauté until fragrant and softened, about 2-3 minutes.
2. Stir in the turmeric, ginger, and cumin, and cook for another minute to release the flavors.
3. Add the carrots and celery to the pot, cooking for 4-5 minutes until slightly softened.
4. Pour in the chicken broth and bring the soup to a gentle boil. Reduce the heat to low and simmer for 10-12 minutes, or until the vegetables are tender.
5. Stir in the shredded chicken and coconut milk, if using. Simmer for an additional 5 minutes, allowing the flavors to meld together.
6. Add the spinach or kale leaves and cook until just wilted, about 1-2 minutes.
7. Stir in the lemon juice and season with salt and pepper to taste.
8. Serve hot, garnished with additional lemon wedges or fresh herbs if desired.

Nutritional Values (per serving):

- Calories: 250
- Fat: 10g
- Carbohydrates: 15g

- Protein: 22g

Lentil & Kale Soup

Ingredients:

- 1 tablespoon olive oil
- 1 medium onion, diced
- 2 carrots, diced
- 2 celery stalks, diced
- 2 cloves garlic, minced
- 1 teaspoon ground cumin
- 1 teaspoon smoked paprika
- 1/2 teaspoon turmeric
- 1 cup dried green or brown lentils, rinsed
- 6 cups vegetable broth or water
- 2 cups chopped kale, stems removed
- 1 can (14 oz) diced tomatoes, with juices
- 1 teaspoon lemon juice
- Salt and pepper to taste
- Optional: fresh parsley or cilantro for garnish

Directions:

1. Heat the olive oil in a large pot over medium heat. Add the onion, carrots, and celery, and sauté until softened, about 5 minutes.
2. Stir in the garlic, cumin, smoked paprika, and turmeric, and cook for 1 minute until fragrant.
3. Add the lentils and stir to coat them with the spices and vegetables.
4. Pour in the vegetable broth or water and bring to a boil. Reduce the heat to low and simmer for 20-25 minutes, or until the lentils are tender.
5. Stir in the chopped kale and canned diced tomatoes. Simmer for an additional 5 minutes until the kale is wilted and the flavors meld together.
6. Add the lemon juice and season with salt and pepper to taste.
7. Serve hot, garnished with fresh parsley or cilantro if desired.

Nutritional Values (per serving):

- Calories: 220
- Fat: 5g
- Carbohydrates: 35g
- Protein: 12g

Chia and Walnut Salad with Avocado and Lemon Vinaigrette

Ingredients:

- 4 cups mixed greens (such as spinach, arugula, and kale)
- 1 ripe avocado, diced
- 1/4 cup walnuts, roughly chopped
- 1 tablespoon chia seeds
- 1/2 cup cherry tomatoes, halved
- 1/4 cup cucumber, thinly sliced
- For the Lemon Vinaigrette:
- 2 tablespoons fresh lemon juice
- 3 tablespoons olive oil
- 1 teaspoon honey or maple syrup (optional)
- 1/2 teaspoon Dijon mustard

- Salt and pepper to taste

Directions:

1. In a large salad bowl, combine the mixed greens, diced avocado, chopped walnuts, chia seeds, cherry tomatoes, and cucumber. Toss gently to mix.
2. In a small bowl, whisk together the lemon juice, olive oil, honey or maple syrup (if using), Dijon mustard, salt, and pepper until emulsified.
3. Drizzle the lemon vinaigrette over the salad and toss gently to coat all the ingredients evenly.
4. Taste and adjust seasoning if needed, adding more lemon juice or salt to your preference.
5. Serve immediately as a light lunch or side dish, garnished with extra walnuts or chia seeds if desired.

Nutritional Values (per serving):

- Calories: 250
- Fat: 20g
- Carbohydrates: 12g
- Protein: 5g

Salmon Salad with Spinach and Walnuts

Ingredients:

- 4 cups fresh spinach leaves
- 1 cooked salmon fillet (4-6 ounces), flaked
- 1/4 cup walnuts, roughly chopped
- 1/4 cup red onion, thinly sliced
- 1/2 avocado, sliced
- 1/2 cup cherry tomatoes, halved
- For the Dressing:
- 2 tablespoons olive oil
- 1 tablespoon fresh lemon juice
- 1 teaspoon Dijon mustard
- 1 teaspoon honey or maple syrup (optional)
- Salt and pepper to taste

Directions:

1. Arrange the spinach leaves in a large salad bowl or on a plate as the base.
2. Top with flaked salmon, chopped walnuts, red onion slices, avocado, and cherry tomatoes.
3. In a small bowl, whisk together olive oil, lemon juice, Dijon mustard, honey or maple syrup (if using), salt, and pepper until smooth and well combined.
4. Drizzle the dressing evenly over the salad. Toss gently to coat all the ingredients or leave undressed for individual serving preferences.
5. Serve immediately and enjoy a fresh, nutrient-packed meal.

Nutritional Values (per serving):

- Calories: 380
- Fat: 27g
- Carbohydrates: 10g
- Protein: 25g

Zucchini Noodles with Pesto & Grilled Chicken

Ingredients:

- 2 medium zucchinis, spiralized into noodles
- 1 boneless, skinless chicken breast
- 1/2 cup fresh basil pesto (store-bought or homemade)
- 1 tablespoon olive oil
- 1/4 cup cherry tomatoes, halved
- 1 tablespoon grated Parmesan cheese (optional)
- Salt and pepper to taste

Directions:

1. Heat a grill pan or outdoor grill over medium-high heat. Season the chicken breast with salt, pepper, and a drizzle of olive oil. Grill for 6-7 minutes per side, or until fully cooked with an internal temperature of 165°F (75°C). Set aside to rest for a few minutes, then slice into strips.
2. Heat the olive oil in a large skillet over medium heat. Add the spiralized zucchini noodles and cook for 2-3 minutes, stirring occasionally, until slightly softened. Avoid overcooking to maintain their crisp texture.
3. Remove the zucchini noodles from the heat and toss them with the basil pesto until evenly coated.
4. Plate the pesto-coated zucchini noodles and top with the grilled chicken strips and halved cherry tomatoes.
5. Sprinkle with Parmesan cheese if desired, and serve immediately.

Nutritional Values (per serving):

- Calories: 310
- Fat: 20g
- Carbohydrates: 10g
- Protein: 25g

Roasted Veggie & Hummus Wrap

Ingredients:

- 1 large whole-grain tortilla or wrap
- 1/2 cup hummus (any flavor of your choice)
- 1/2 cup zucchini, sliced
- 1/2 cup red bell pepper, sliced
- 1/2 cup eggplant, sliced
- 1/4 cup red onion, sliced
- 1 tablespoon olive oil
- 1 teaspoon smoked paprika or cumin (optional)
- Salt and pepper to taste
- Optional toppings: fresh spinach or arugula

Directions:

1. Preheat your oven to 400°F (200°C). Toss the zucchini, red bell pepper, eggplant, and red onion with olive oil, smoked paprika or cumin (if using), salt, and pepper. Spread the vegetables evenly on a baking sheet.
2. Roast in the oven for 20-25 minutes, turning halfway through,

until the vegetables are tender and slightly caramelized. Remove from the oven and let cool slightly.
3. Lay the whole-grain tortilla flat and spread a generous layer of hummus over the surface.
4. Arrange the roasted vegetables in the center of the tortilla. If desired, add a handful of fresh spinach or arugula for an extra crunch and flavor boost.
5. Fold in the sides of the tortilla and roll it tightly into a wrap. Slice in half if desired, and serve immediately.

Nutritional Values (per serving):

- Calories: 320
- Fat: 15g
- Carbohydrates: 38g
- Protein: 8g

Shrimp & Avocado Lettuce Wraps

Ingredients:

- 1/2 pound cooked shrimp, peeled and deveined
- 1 avocado, diced
- 8 large lettuce leaves (such as romaine or butter lettuce)
- 1/4 cup cherry tomatoes, diced
- 2 tablespoons fresh cilantro, chopped
- 1 tablespoon lime juice
- 1 teaspoon olive oil
- Salt and pepper to taste
- Optional toppings: a sprinkle of red pepper flakes or a drizzle of hot sauce

Directions:

1. In a medium bowl, combine the cooked shrimp, diced avocado, cherry tomatoes, cilantro, lime juice, and olive oil. Toss gently to coat all the ingredients without mashing the avocado. Season with salt and pepper to taste.
2. Lay the lettuce leaves flat on a plate or serving platter.
3. Spoon the shrimp and avocado mixture evenly into each lettuce leaf, folding the leaves slightly to create wraps.
4. Add optional toppings such as red pepper flakes or hot sauce for an extra kick.
5. Serve immediately as a light, fresh meal or appetizer.

Nutritional Values (per serving):

- Calories: 250
- Fat: 15g
- Carbohydrates: 10g
- Protein: 20g

Miso Soup with Tofu and Seaweed

Ingredients:

- 4 cups water
- 3 tablespoons white miso paste
- 1/2 cup cubed firm tofu
- 1/4 cup dried wakame seaweed
- 2 green onions, thinly sliced

- 1/2 cup sliced mushrooms (optional)
- 1 tablespoon soy sauce (optional, for additional flavor)

Directions:

1. In a medium saucepan, bring the water to a gentle simmer over medium heat.
2. Add the wakame seaweed and let it rehydrate in the simmering water for about 2-3 minutes until it expands.
3. Lower the heat and stir in the miso paste using a ladle or whisk. Stir gently to ensure the miso dissolves completely without boiling, as boiling can affect the flavor of the miso.
4. Add the tofu cubes and sliced mushrooms (if using) to the soup. Simmer for 2-3 minutes to warm the tofu and slightly soften the mushrooms.
5. Stir in the soy sauce if desired and adjust the seasoning to taste.
6. Serve the soup hot, garnished with sliced green onions.

Nutritional Values (per serving):

- Calories: 120
- Fat: 4g
- Carbohydrates: 10g
- Protein: 10g

Quinoa & Black Bean Buddha Bowl

Ingredients:

- 1 cup cooked quinoa
- 1/2 cup black beans, rinsed and drained
- 1/2 cup cherry tomatoes, halved
- 1/2 cup diced cucumber
- 1/4 cup shredded carrots
- 1/2 avocado, sliced
- 2 tablespoons fresh cilantro, chopped
- 1 tablespoon olive oil
- 1 tablespoon fresh lime juice
- 1/2 teaspoon cumin
- Salt and pepper to taste
- Optional toppings: a dollop of Greek yogurt or a drizzle of hot sauce

Directions:

1. In a medium bowl, toss the cooked quinoa with olive oil, lime juice, cumin, salt, and pepper to season it.
2. Arrange the quinoa in a serving bowl as the base.
3. Layer the black beans, cherry tomatoes, cucumber, shredded carrots, and avocado slices over the quinoa.
4. Sprinkle the fresh cilantro on top for added flavor.
5. Add optional toppings like Greek yogurt or hot sauce for extra creaminess or spice.

6. Serve immediately as a colorful and nutrient-packed lunch or dinner.

Nutritional Values (per serving):

- Calories: 330
- Fat: 15g
- Carbohydrates: 38g
- Protein: 10g

Eggplant & Lentil Stew

Ingredients:

- 1 medium eggplant, diced
- 1 cup cooked lentils (green or brown)
- 1 can (14 oz) diced tomatoes, with juices
- 1 small onion, diced
- 2 cloves garlic, minced
- 1 tablespoon olive oil
- 1 teaspoon ground cumin
- 1/2 teaspoon smoked paprika
- 1/4 teaspoon cayenne pepper (optional, for heat)
- 2 cups vegetable broth
- Salt and pepper to taste
- 2 tablespoons fresh parsley or cilantro, chopped (for garnish)

Directions:

1. Heat the olive oil in a large pot over medium heat. Add the onion and garlic, and sauté until fragrant and softened, about 3-4 minutes.
2. Stir in the diced eggplant, cumin, smoked paprika, and cayenne pepper if using. Cook for 5-7 minutes, stirring occasionally, until the eggplant begins to soften.
3. Add the diced tomatoes and vegetable broth. Bring the mixture to a boil, then reduce the heat to low and let it simmer for 15 minutes, allowing the eggplant to become tender.
4. Stir in the cooked lentils and season the stew with salt and pepper to taste. Simmer for an additional 5 minutes to combine the flavors.
5. Serve hot, garnished with fresh parsley or cilantro for a bright, herbal finish.

Nutritional Values (per serving):

- Calories: 220
- Fat: 5g
- Carbohydrates: 35g
- Protein: 10g

Grilled Chicken Caesar Salad with Greek Yogurt Dressing

Ingredients:

- 1 boneless, skinless chicken breast
- 6 cups chopped romaine lettuce
- 1/4 cup Parmesan cheese, grated
- 1/2 cup whole-grain croutons (optional)
- 1 tablespoon olive oil
- Salt and pepper to taste
- For the Greek Yogurt Dressing:
- 1/2 cup plain Greek yogurt
- 1 tablespoon olive oil
- 1 tablespoon fresh lemon juice

- 1 teaspoon Dijon mustard
- 1 teaspoon Worcestershire sauce
- 1 clove garlic, minced
- 1 tablespoon grated Parmesan cheese
- Salt and pepper to taste

Directions:

1. Preheat a grill or grill pan over medium-high heat. Season the chicken breast with olive oil, salt, and pepper. Grill for 6-7 minutes per side or until fully cooked with an internal temperature of 165°F (75°C). Set aside to rest for a few minutes, then slice into strips.
2. To prepare the dressing, whisk together the Greek yogurt, olive oil, lemon juice, Dijon mustard, Worcestershire sauce, minced garlic, grated Parmesan, salt, and pepper in a small bowl until smooth and creamy.
3. In a large salad bowl, toss the chopped romaine lettuce with half of the Greek yogurt dressing to coat the leaves evenly.
4. Arrange the grilled chicken strips on top of the dressed lettuce. Sprinkle with grated Parmesan cheese and add croutons if desired.
5. Drizzle the remaining dressing over the salad or serve it on the side.
6. Serve immediately as a hearty and flavorful lunch or dinner.

Nutritional Values (per serving):

- Calories: 320
- Fat: 15g
- Carbohydrates: 12g
- Protein: 35g

Salmon & Broccoli Stir-Fry

Ingredients:

- 2 salmon fillets (about 6 ounces each), cut into bite-sized pieces
- 2 cups broccoli florets
- 1 red bell pepper, thinly sliced
- 2 tablespoons soy sauce or tamari (for a gluten-free option)
- 1 tablespoon honey or maple syrup
- 1 tablespoon sesame oil (or olive oil)
- 1 teaspoon grated ginger
- 1 clove garlic, minced
- 1 tablespoon sesame seeds (optional, for garnish)
- Salt and pepper to taste

Directions:

1. In a small bowl, whisk together the soy sauce, honey or maple syrup, grated ginger, and minced garlic. Set aside.
2. Heat the sesame oil in a large skillet or wok over medium-high heat. Add the broccoli florets and red bell pepper, cooking for 3-4 minutes until they begin to soften but remain crisp. Remove the vegetables from the skillet and set aside.

3. Add the salmon pieces to the same skillet. Cook for 2-3 minutes on each side until they are lightly browned and cooked through.
4. Return the vegetables to the skillet with the salmon. Pour the sauce over the mixture and gently toss to coat evenly. Cook for an additional 1-2 minutes to heat through and meld the flavors.
5. Serve immediately, garnished with sesame seeds if desired.

Nutritional Values (per serving):

- Calories: 320
- Fat: 16g
- Carbohydrates: 12g
- Protein: 35g

Cabbage & Carrot Slaw with Avocado

Ingredients:

- 2 cups shredded cabbage (green, purple, or a mix)
- 1 cup shredded carrots
- 1 ripe avocado, diced
- 2 tablespoons fresh cilantro, chopped (optional)
- 1 tablespoon lime juice
- 1 tablespoon olive oil
- Salt and pepper to taste
- Optional toppings: pumpkin seeds or a sprinkle of red pepper flakes

Directions:

1. In a large mixing bowl, combine the shredded cabbage and carrots. Toss to mix evenly.
2. Add the diced avocado and gently fold it into the cabbage and carrot mixture, taking care not to mash the avocado.
3. In a small bowl, whisk together the lime juice, olive oil, salt, and pepper.
4. Pour the dressing over the slaw and toss gently until all the ingredients are coated.
5. Garnish with fresh cilantro and optional toppings such as pumpkin seeds or red pepper flakes for added flavor and crunch.
6. Serve immediately as a fresh and vibrant side dish or light lunch.

Nutritional Values (per serving):

- Calories: 200
- Fat: 15g
- Carbohydrates: 14g
- Protein: 3g

Grilled Veggie & Halloumi Salad

Ingredients:

- 1 medium zucchini, sliced into rounds
- 1 red bell pepper, cut into strips
- 1 small eggplant, sliced into rounds
- 6 ounces halloumi cheese, sliced
- 4 cups mixed greens (such as arugula, spinach, or lettuce)
- 2 tablespoons olive oil
- 1 tablespoon balsamic vinegar
- 1 teaspoon dried oregano
- Salt and pepper to taste

- Optional toppings:
- Cherry tomatoes, sliced
- Toasted pine nuts

Directions:

1. Preheat a grill or grill pan over medium-high heat. Brush the zucchini, red bell pepper, and eggplant slices with 1 tablespoon of olive oil. Sprinkle with salt, pepper, and oregano.
2. Grill the vegetables for 3-4 minutes per side, or until they are tender and have visible grill marks. Remove and set aside.
3. Add the halloumi slices to the grill and cook for 1-2 minutes per side, or until golden brown and slightly crispy. Remove from the grill and set aside.
4. In a small bowl, whisk together the remaining olive oil and balsamic vinegar to make the dressing.
5. In a large salad bowl or platter, arrange the mixed greens as the base. Top with the grilled vegetables and halloumi slices.
6. Drizzle the balsamic dressing over the salad and garnish with optional toppings like cherry tomatoes or toasted pine nuts if desired.
7. Serve immediately while the halloumi is warm.

Nutritional Values (per serving):

- Calories: 320
- Fat: 22g
- Carbohydrates: 12g
- Protein: 15g

Sweet Potato & Black Bean Chili

Ingredients:

- 1 large sweet potato, peeled and diced
- 1 can (15 oz) black beans, drained and rinsed
- 1 can (14.5 oz) diced tomatoes
- 1 onion, chopped
- 2 cloves garlic, minced
- 1 bell pepper, chopped
- 2 tablespoons chili powder
- 1 teaspoon cumin
- 1/2 teaspoon smoked paprika
- 1/4 teaspoon cayenne pepper (adjust to taste)
- 3 cups vegetable broth
- 2 tablespoons olive oil
- Salt and pepper to taste
- Optional toppings: chopped cilantro, diced avocado, shredded cheese, sour cream

Directions:

1. Heat olive oil in a large pot over medium heat. Add the onion and bell pepper, sautéing until they begin to soften, about 3-4 minutes.
2. Add the garlic, chili powder, cumin, smoked paprika, and cayenne pepper. Cook for another minute until the spices are fragrant.
3. Stir in the sweet potatoes, black beans, and diced tomatoes with their juices. Pour in the vegetable

broth and bring the mixture to a simmer.
4. Reduce heat to low and let the chili simmer, partially covered, for about 25-30 minutes, or until the sweet potatoes are tender and the chili has thickened.
5. Season with salt and pepper to taste. Serve hot, with optional toppings like cilantro, avocado, cheese, or sour cream.

Nutritional Values (per serving):

- Calories: 280
- Fat: 7g
- Carbohydrates: 47g
- Protein: 10g

Coconut & Lime Chicken with Mango Salad

Ingredients:

- 2 boneless, skinless chicken breasts
- 1 cup coconut milk
- Juice of 2 limes
- 1 tablespoon honey
- 1 teaspoon chili flakes (adjust to taste)
- Salt and pepper to taste
- 1 ripe mango, diced
- 1/2 red bell pepper, finely chopped
- 1/4 red onion, finely chopped
- 1/4 cup fresh cilantro, chopped
- 1 tablespoon olive oil
- 1 tablespoon lime juice (additional for salad dressing)

- For the Chicken Marinade:
- 1/2 cup coconut milk
- Juice of 1 lime
- 1/2 tablespoon honey
- Salt and pepper

Directions:

1. Marinate the Chicken: In a bowl, combine 1/2 cup coconut milk, juice of 1 lime, 1/2 tablespoon honey, salt, and pepper. Whisk until well mixed. Add the chicken breasts, making sure they are fully submerged in the marinade. Cover and refrigerate for at least 1 hour, or overnight for more flavor.
2. Prepare the Mango Salad: In a separate bowl, mix the diced mango, red bell pepper, red onion, and cilantro. In a small cup, whisk together olive oil and 1 tablespoon of lime juice to create a light dressing. Pour the dressing over the mango salad, toss gently, and set aside.
3. Cook the Chicken: Heat a grill pan or skillet over medium heat. Remove the chicken from the marinade, letting the excess drip off. Grill the chicken for 6-7 minutes on each side, or until fully cooked and the internal temperature reaches 165°F (74°C). During the last few minutes of cooking, baste the chicken with the remaining 1 cup of coconut milk mixed with 1 tablespoon of honey,

lime juice, and chili flakes to create a glaze.
4. Serve: Slice the grilled chicken and serve alongside the fresh mango salad. Drizzle any remaining glaze over the chicken if desired.

Nutritional Values (per serving):

- Calories: 450
- Fat: 18g
- Carbohydrates: 35g
- Protein: 38g

Turkey & Avocado Lettuce Wraps

Ingredients:

- 1 pound ground turkey
- 1 ripe avocado, diced
- 8-10 large lettuce leaves (such as butter lettuce or romaine)
- 1/2 red onion, finely diced
- 1 tomato, diced
- 1 teaspoon garlic powder
- 1 teaspoon cumin
- Salt and pepper to taste
- 2 tablespoons olive oil
- Optional: lime wedges for serving, cilantro for garnish, and a dollop of Greek yogurt or sour cream

Directions:

1. Heat olive oil in a skillet over medium heat. Add the ground turkey and cook, stirring and breaking up the meat with a spatula, until browned and cooked through, about 5-7 minutes.
2. Season the turkey with garlic powder, cumin, salt, and pepper during cooking to enhance the flavor.
3. In a bowl, combine the cooked turkey, diced avocado, red onion, and tomato. Gently toss everything together, being careful not to mash the avocado.
4. Arrange the lettuce leaves on a platter. Spoon the turkey and avocado mixture into the center of each lettuce leaf.
5. If desired, garnish with fresh cilantro, add a squeeze of lime juice, and a dollop of Greek yogurt or sour cream on top of each wrap.
6. Serve immediately, allowing guests to enjoy the wraps while the filling is still warm.

Nutritional Values (per serving):

- Calories: 320
- Fat: 18g
- Carbohydrates: 8g
- Protein: 28g

Spicy Quinoa & Vegetable Stir-Fry

Ingredients:

- 1 cup cooked quinoa
- 1 tablespoon olive oil
- 1 red bell pepper, thinly sliced
- 1 cup broccoli florets
- 1 carrot, julienned
- 1 small zucchini, sliced
- 2 cloves garlic, minced
- 1 tablespoon fresh ginger, minced

- 2 tablespoons soy sauce
- 1 tablespoon chili sauce or sriracha
- 1 teaspoon sesame oil
- Optional: sesame seeds and sliced green onions for garnish

Directions:

1. Heat the olive oil in a large skillet or wok over medium-high heat. Add the garlic and ginger, sautéing for about 30 seconds until fragrant.
2. Add the red bell pepper, broccoli, carrot, and zucchini to the skillet. Stir-fry for about 5-7 minutes, or until the vegetables are tender-crisp.
3. Stir in the cooked quinoa, soy sauce, chili sauce, and sesame oil. Mix well to combine all the ingredients and coat everything evenly with the sauce.
4. Continue to stir-fry for an additional 2-3 minutes, allowing the quinoa to absorb the flavors and heat through.
5. Remove from heat and garnish with sesame seeds and sliced green onions if desired.
6. Serve hot as a flavorful and spicy main dish that combines the nutritional benefits of quinoa with a medley of vegetables.

Nutritional Values (per serving):

- Calories: 280
- Fat: 10g
- Carbohydrates: 40g
- Protein: 8g

Grilled Tofu with Spinach & Pine Nuts

Ingredients:

- 1 block (14 oz) firm tofu, pressed and sliced
- 2 tablespoons olive oil
- 2 cloves garlic, minced
- 4 cups fresh spinach
- 1/4 cup pine nuts
- 2 tablespoons soy sauce
- 1 tablespoon balsamic vinegar
- Salt and pepper to taste
- Optional: lemon wedges for serving

Directions:

1. Preheat your grill or grill pan over medium-high heat. Brush the tofu slices with 1 tablespoon of olive oil and season lightly with salt and pepper.
2. Place tofu slices on the grill and cook for about 3-4 minutes on each side, or until they have nice grill marks and are heated through.
3. Meanwhile, heat the remaining tablespoon of olive oil in a skillet over medium heat. Add the minced garlic and sauté for about 1 minute until fragrant.
4. Add the spinach to the skillet and cook until just wilted, about 2-3 minutes.

5. Stir in the pine nuts, soy sauce, and balsamic vinegar, and season with salt and pepper to taste. Cook for an additional 1-2 minutes to allow the flavors to meld.
6. Serve the grilled tofu topped with the spinach and pine nut mixture. Optionally, squeeze a lemon wedge over each serving to add a refreshing zest.

Nutritional Values (per serving):

- Calories: 280
- Fat: 18g
- Carbohydrates: 10g
- Protein: 20g

Chickpea & Sweet Potato Buddha Bowl

Ingredients:

- 1 large sweet potato, peeled and cubed
- 1 can (15 oz) chickpeas, drained, rinsed, and patted dry
- 2 cups cooked quinoa
- 2 cups mixed greens (such as spinach, kale, or arugula)
- 1/4 cup red onion, thinly sliced
- 1/4 cup tahini
- 2 tablespoons lemon juice
- 2 tablespoons olive oil
- 1 teaspoon ground cumin
- 1/2 teaspoon paprika
- Salt and pepper to taste
- Optional garnishes: avocado slices, sesame seeds, fresh cilantro

Directions:

1. Preheat your oven to 400°F (200°C). Toss the sweet potato cubes with 1 tablespoon of olive oil, cumin, paprika, salt, and pepper. Spread them on a baking sheet and roast for 25-30 minutes, or until tender and slightly caramelized.
2. On a separate baking sheet, spread the chickpeas and toss them with the remaining olive oil and a pinch of salt. Roast in the oven alongside the sweet potatoes for 20-25 minutes, shaking the pan occasionally, until crispy.
3. In a small bowl, whisk together the tahini, lemon juice, and 2-3 tablespoons of water to achieve a drizzling consistency. Season with salt and pepper.
4. To assemble the bowls, divide the cooked quinoa among four bowls. Top each with mixed greens, roasted sweet potatoes, crispy chickpeas, and sliced red onion.
5. Drizzle each bowl generously with the tahini lemon dressing.
6. Garnish with optional toppings like avocado slices, sesame seeds, or fresh cilantro.
7. Serve immediately, enjoying a blend of flavors and textures that make this Buddha bowl both nutritious and satisfying.

Nutritional Values (per serving):

- Calories: 450
- Fat: 18g
- Carbohydrates: 62g
- Protein: 14g

Asian-Inspired Salmon Salad

Ingredients:

- 2 salmon fillets (about 6 ounces each)
- 4 cups mixed greens (such as baby spinach, arugula, and romaine lettuce)
- 1 cup shredded carrots
- 1 red bell pepper, thinly sliced
- 1/2 cucumber, thinly sliced
- 1/4 cup fresh cilantro, chopped
- 2 tablespoons sesame seeds
- 2 tablespoons soy sauce
- 1 tablespoon sesame oil
- 1 tablespoon rice vinegar
- 1 tablespoon honey
- 1 teaspoon grated ginger
- 1 clove garlic, minced
- Optional: crushed peanuts or sliced green onions for garnish

Directions:

1. Preheat your grill or grill pan over medium heat. Season the salmon fillets with salt and pepper, and grill for about 4-5 minutes on each side or until cooked through and easily flaked with a fork. Set aside to cool slightly.
2. In a large salad bowl, combine the mixed greens, shredded carrots, sliced red bell pepper, cucumber, and cilantro.
3. In a small bowl, whisk together the soy sauce, sesame oil, rice vinegar, honey, grated ginger, and minced garlic to create the dressing.
4. Flake the grilled salmon into large pieces and add them to the salad.
5. Drizzle the dressing over the salad and toss gently to coat all the ingredients evenly.
6. Sprinkle sesame seeds over the top and add optional garnishes like crushed peanuts or sliced green onions if desired.
7. Serve the salad immediately, offering a refreshing and flavorful blend of textures and tastes.

Nutritional Values (per serving):

- Calories: 420
- Fat: 22g
- Carbohydrates: 18g
- Protein: 35g

Cauliflower Rice Stir-Fry with Vegetables

Ingredients:

- 1 medium head of cauliflower, grated or processed into rice-sized pieces
- 2 tablespoons olive oil
- 1 red bell pepper, thinly sliced

- 1 cup snap peas, trimmed
- 1 carrot, thinly sliced
- 1 small onion, thinly sliced
- 2 cloves garlic, minced
- 1 tablespoon soy sauce
- 1 tablespoon hoisin sauce (optional, for added sweetness and depth)
- 1 teaspoon sesame oil
- Salt and pepper to taste
- Optional garnishes: sliced green onions, sesame seeds

Directions:

1. Heat one tablespoon of olive oil in a large skillet or wok over medium-high heat. Add the onion and garlic, sautéing until the onion becomes translucent and the garlic is fragrant, about 2 minutes.
2. Add the remaining vegetables: red bell pepper, snap peas, and carrot. Stir-fry for about 3-5 minutes until the vegetables are just tender but still crisp.
3. Push the vegetables to the side of the skillet and add the remaining tablespoon of olive oil. Pour the cauliflower rice into the center of the skillet and stir to combine it with the vegetables.
4. Stir in the soy sauce, hoisin sauce if using, and sesame oil. Cook, stirring frequently, for an additional 5-7 minutes, until the cauliflower rice is tender and everything is heated through.
5. Season with salt and pepper to taste. Remove from heat.
6. Serve hot, garnished with green onions and sesame seeds if desired.

Nutritional Values (per serving):

- Calories: 180
- Fat: 10g
- Carbohydrates: 18g
- Protein: 4g

Dinner

Dinner is a time to unwind and savor the flavors of carefully crafted dishes that not only satisfy your hunger but also enhance your well-being. In this chapter, you'll discover 25 dinner recipes that are both nourishing and delightful. Each recipe is designed to support hormonal balance, reduce stress, and promote overall health with a variety of ingredients rich in nutrients. From cozy soups and vibrant stir-fries to hearty entrees and light, refreshing salads, these dishes cater to diverse tastes and dietary preferences, ensuring that every meal is an opportunity to treat your body and taste buds to something special.

Grilled Salmon with Roasted Brussels Sprouts and Quinoa

Ingredients:

- 2 salmon fillets (about 6 ounces each)
- 1 cup quinoa
- 2 cups Brussels sprouts, halved
- 2 tablespoons olive oil
- Salt and pepper to taste
- Lemon wedges for serving

For the marinade:

- 2 tablespoons soy sauce
- 1 tablespoon honey
- 1 tablespoon olive oil
- 1 clove garlic, minced
- 1 teaspoon lemon zest

Directions:

1. Preheat the oven to 400°F (200°C) for roasting the Brussels sprouts. Cook the quinoa according to package instructions. Typically, rinse 1 cup of quinoa and cook in 2 cups of water for about 15 minutes or until the water is absorbed and the quinoa is tender.
2. Prepare the marinade by whisking together soy sauce, honey, olive oil, minced garlic, and lemon zest in a small bowl. Place the salmon fillets in a shallow dish or zip-lock bag, pour the marinade over the salmon, and let marinate in the refrigerator for at least 30 minutes.
3. Roast the Brussels sprouts: Toss the Brussels sprouts with 2 tablespoons of olive oil, salt, and pepper. Spread them out on a baking sheet and roast in the preheated oven for about 20-25 minutes, or until they are crispy on the outside and tender on the inside.
4. Grill the salmon: Heat a grill or grill pan over medium-high heat. Remove the salmon from the marinade, letting excess drip off. Grill the salmon for about 4-5

minutes on each side or until cooked through and easily flaked with a fork.
5. Assemble and serve: Place a scoop of cooked quinoa on each plate, top with a grilled salmon fillet, and surround with roasted Brussels sprouts. Serve with lemon wedges for added flavor.

Nutritional Values (per serving):

- Calories: 560
- Fat: 30g
- Carbohydrates: 40g
- Protein: 35g

Turmeric and Ginger Chicken Stir-Fry

Ingredients:

- 2 boneless, skinless chicken breasts, thinly sliced
- 1 tablespoon olive oil
- 1 medium bell pepper, sliced
- 1 medium carrot, julienned
- 1 cup broccoli florets
- 1 small onion, sliced
- 2 cloves garlic, minced
- 1 tablespoon fresh ginger, grated
- 1 teaspoon turmeric powder
- 2 tablespoons soy sauce
- 1 tablespoon oyster sauce (optional)
- Salt and pepper to taste
- Fresh cilantro or green onions for garnish

Directions:

1. Heat oil in a large skillet or wok over medium-high heat. Add the sliced chicken breasts and stir-fry until they are lightly browned and cooked through, about 5-6 minutes. Remove the chicken from the pan and set aside.
2. In the same skillet, add a little more oil if necessary, and sauté the onion, garlic, and ginger until fragrant, about 1-2 minutes. Add the bell pepper, carrot, and broccoli, and continue to stir-fry for another 3-4 minutes until the vegetables are just tender but still crisp.
3. Return the chicken to the skillet. Sprinkle the turmeric over the chicken and vegetables, stirring well to coat everything evenly. Pour in the soy sauce and oyster sauce (if using), and season with salt and pepper. Stir well to combine all ingredients and ensure the chicken and vegetables are evenly coated with the sauces and spices.
4. Cook for an additional 2-3 minutes, stirring frequently, until everything is heated through and the flavors have melded together.
5. Garnish with fresh cilantro or sliced green onions before serving. This dish is great on its own or can be served over rice or noodles for a more filling meal.

Nutritional Values (per serving):

- Calories: 320
- Fat: 10g
- Carbohydrates: 15g
- Protein: 40g

Spaghetti Squash with Pesto and Grilled Chicken

Ingredients:

- 1 medium spaghetti squash
- 2 boneless, skinless chicken breasts
- 1/2 cup homemade or store-bought pesto
- 2 tablespoons olive oil
- Salt and pepper to taste
- Grated Parmesan cheese, for serving
- Fresh basil leaves, for garnish

Directions:

1. Preheat your oven to 400°F (200°C). Cut the spaghetti squash in half lengthwise and scoop out the seeds. Drizzle with 1 tablespoon of olive oil and season with salt and pepper. Place cut-side down on a baking sheet and roast in the oven for 40-50 minutes, or until the flesh is easily shredded with a fork.
2. While the squash is roasting, prepare the chicken. Season the chicken breasts with salt and pepper. Heat the remaining tablespoon of olive oil in a grill pan over medium-high heat. Grill the chicken for about 6-7 minutes on each side, or until fully cooked and the internal temperature reaches 165°F (74°C). Let the chicken rest for a few minutes before slicing it thinly.
3. When the spaghetti squash is cooked, use a fork to scrape the insides into strands that resemble spaghetti noodles. Transfer the spaghetti squash strands to a large mixing bowl.
4. Toss the spaghetti squash strands with pesto, ensuring they are evenly coated. Adjust the seasoning with more salt and pepper if needed.
5. Serve the pesto spaghetti squash topped with sliced grilled chicken. Garnish with grated Parmesan cheese and fresh basil leaves for added flavor.

Nutritional Values (per serving):

- Calories: 510
- Fat: 30g
- Carbohydrates: 28g
- Protein: 35g

Lemon & Herb Baked Cod with Steamed Vegetables

Ingredients:

- 4 cod fillets (about 6 ounces each)
- 2 tablespoons olive oil
- Juice and zest of 1 lemon
- 2 cloves garlic, minced

- 1 tablespoon fresh parsley, chopped
- 1 tablespoon fresh dill, chopped
- Salt and pepper to taste
- Assorted vegetables for steaming (such as broccoli, carrots, and green beans)

Directions:

1. Preheat your oven to 400°F (200°C). Prepare a baking dish by lightly greasing it with some of the olive oil.
2. Prepare the lemon herb mixture. In a small bowl, combine the remaining olive oil, lemon juice, lemon zest, minced garlic, chopped parsley, and dill. Stir well to mix. Season the mixture with salt and pepper to your liking.
3. Prepare the cod fillets. Place the cod fillets in the prepared baking dish. Spoon the lemon herb mixture evenly over each fillet, ensuring they are well coated.
4. Bake the cod. Place the baking dish in the preheated oven and bake for 12-15 minutes, or until the cod is opaque and flakes easily with a fork.
5. Steam the vegetables. While the cod is baking, steam the chosen vegetables until they are just tender. This should take about 7-10 minutes depending on the vegetables used.
6. Serve the dish. Once the cod is cooked and the vegetables are steamed, serve the cod immediately alongside the steamed vegetables.

Nutritional Values (per serving):

- Calories: 220
- Fat: 7g
- Carbohydrates: 5g
- Protein: 35g

Zucchini Noodles with Avocado Pesto

Ingredients:

- 4 medium zucchinis, spiralized into noodles
- 1 ripe avocado
- 1/2 cup fresh basil leaves
- 2 cloves garlic
- 2 tablespoons pine nuts (plus extra for garnish)
- 2 tablespoons lemon juice
- 1/4 cup olive oil
- Salt and pepper to taste
- Grated Parmesan cheese for serving (optional)

Directions:

1. Prepare the avocado pesto. In a food processor, combine the avocado, basil leaves, garlic, pine nuts, and lemon juice. Pulse until the ingredients are roughly chopped. With the processor running, slowly pour in the olive oil and continue to process until the mixture is smooth and creamy. Season with salt and pepper to taste.

2. Cook the zucchini noodles. Heat a large skillet over medium heat. Add the spiralized zucchini noodles and cook for 2-3 minutes, just until warmed through and slightly softened. Be careful not to overcook the noodles to avoid them becoming too soft or watery.
3. Combine the noodles and pesto. Remove the skillet from heat. Add the avocado pesto to the zucchini noodles and gently toss to combine, ensuring the noodles are evenly coated.
4. Serve. Plate the zucchini noodles and garnish with additional pine nuts and grated Parmesan cheese if desired. Serve immediately.

Nutritional Values (per serving):

- Calories: 290
- Fat: 25g
- Carbohydrates: 15g
- Protein: 5g

Grilled Chicken with Asparagus and Sweet Potato

Ingredients:

- 4 boneless, skinless chicken breasts
- 1 bunch asparagus, ends trimmed
- 2 medium sweet potatoes, peeled and sliced into 1/2-inch thick rounds
- 2 tablespoons olive oil
- Salt and pepper to taste
- Optional: garlic powder or herbs like rosemary or thyme for extra flavor

Directions:

1. Preheat your grill to medium-high heat.
2. Prepare the vegetables: Toss the asparagus and sweet potato slices with one tablespoon of olive oil, and season with salt, pepper, and any additional herbs or spices if desired.
3. Grill the sweet potatoes: Place the sweet potato slices on the grill, and cook for about 5-7 minutes on each side, or until they are tender and have nice grill marks. Remove from the grill and set aside.
4. Grill the chicken: While the sweet potatoes are grilling, brush the chicken breasts with the remaining tablespoon of olive oil and season with salt, pepper, and any additional desired seasonings. Place the chicken on the grill and cook for 6-8 minutes on each side, or until the chicken is thoroughly cooked and reaches an internal temperature of 165°F (74°C).
5. Add the asparagus: During the last 3-4 minutes of the chicken cooking, add the asparagus to the grill. Cook, turning occasionally, until the asparagus is tender and lightly charred.
6. Serve: Arrange a serving of grilled sweet potatoes and asparagus on

each plate, along with a grilled chicken breast. Serve hot.

Nutritional Values (per serving):

- Calories: 400
- Fat: 12g
- Carbohydrates: 33g
- Protein: 42g

Cauliflower & Chickpea Curry

Ingredients:

- 1 medium head of cauliflower, cut into florets
- 1 can (15 oz) chickpeas, drained and rinsed
- 1 large onion, finely chopped
- 2 cloves garlic, minced
- 1 inch piece of ginger, minced
- 1 can (14 oz) coconut milk
- 2 tablespoons tomato paste
- 2 tablespoons curry powder
- 1 teaspoon turmeric
- 1/2 teaspoon cumin
- 1/2 teaspoon chili powder (adjust based on heat preference)
- Salt and pepper to taste
- 2 tablespoons vegetable oil
- Fresh cilantro, chopped for garnish
- Cooked rice or naan bread for serving

Directions:

1. Sauté the aromatics: Heat the vegetable oil in a large skillet or saucepan over medium heat. Add the onion, garlic, and ginger, cooking until the onion is translucent and fragrant, about 5-7 minutes.
2. Add spices: Stir in the curry powder, turmeric, cumin, chili powder, and tomato paste. Cook for another 1-2 minutes, until the spices are well combined and aromatic.
3. Cook cauliflower and chickpeas: Add the cauliflower florets and chickpeas to the pan, stirring well to coat them with the spice mixture. Cook for about 2-3 minutes.
4. Simmer: Pour in the coconut milk and season with salt and pepper. Bring the mixture to a boil, then reduce the heat and simmer for 15-20 minutes, or until the cauliflower is tender and the curry is thickened.
5. Garnish and serve: Sprinkle chopped cilantro over the curry just before serving. Serve hot with cooked rice or warm naan bread.

Nutritional Values (per serving):

- Calories: 320
- Fat: 18g
- Carbohydrates: 29g
- Protein: 9g

Shrimp Stir-Fry with Bok Choy and Bell Peppers

Ingredients:

- 1 pound shrimp, peeled and deveined
- 2 cups bok choy, chopped
- 1 red bell pepper, thinly sliced
- 1 yellow bell pepper, thinly sliced
- 2 cloves garlic, minced
- 1 tablespoon fresh ginger, minced
- 2 tablespoons soy sauce
- 1 tablespoon oyster sauce
- 1 teaspoon sesame oil
- 2 tablespoons vegetable oil
- Salt and pepper to taste
- Optional: sesame seeds and sliced green onions for garnish

Directions:

1. Heat the vegetable oil in a large skillet or wok over medium-high heat. Add the minced garlic and ginger, and sauté for about 30 seconds until fragrant.
2. Add the bell peppers to the skillet and stir-fry for about 2 minutes, or until they start to soften but still retain some crunch.
3. Include the shrimp to the skillet and stir-fry for about 2-3 minutes, or until they turn pink and are cooked through.
4. Mix in the bok choy, and continue to stir-fry for an additional 2 minutes until the bok choy is wilted but still vibrant.
5. Stir in the soy sauce, oyster sauce, and sesame oil, mixing well to ensure all the ingredients are evenly coated. Season with salt and pepper to taste.
6. Garnish the stir-fry with sesame seeds and sliced green onions if desired.
7. Serve hot, ideally over a bed of steamed rice or noodles for a complete meal.

Nutritional Values (per serving):

- Calories: 240
- Fat: 10g
- Carbohydrates: 8g
- Protein: 26g

Spaghetti Squash Primavera

Ingredients:

- 1 medium spaghetti squash
- 1 tablespoon olive oil
- 1 cup cherry tomatoes, halved
- 1 medium zucchini, diced
- 1 medium yellow squash, diced
- 1 red bell pepper, diced
- 2 cloves garlic, minced
- 1/2 teaspoon Italian seasoning
- 1/4 teaspoon red pepper flakes (optional)
- 1/4 cup grated Parmesan cheese (optional)
- Salt and pepper to taste
- Fresh basil leaves for garnish

Directions:

1. Prepare the spaghetti squash: Preheat your oven to 400°F (200°C). Cut the spaghetti squash in half lengthwise and scoop out the seeds. Drizzle the insides with 1/2 tablespoon olive oil, season with salt and pepper, and place cut-side down on a baking sheet. Roast for 40-50 minutes, or until the flesh is tender and easily shredded with a fork.
2. Cook the vegetables: While the squash is roasting, heat the remaining olive oil in a large skillet over medium heat. Add the garlic and sauté until fragrant, about 1 minute.
3. Add the vegetables: Stir in the cherry tomatoes, zucchini, yellow squash, and red bell pepper. Season with Italian seasoning, red pepper flakes (if using), salt, and pepper. Cook for 5-7 minutes, stirring occasionally, until the vegetables are tender but still vibrant.
4. Assemble the dish: Once the spaghetti squash is cooked, use a fork to scrape the flesh into spaghetti-like strands. Divide the squash among serving plates or bowls. Top with the cooked vegetables and gently toss to combine.
5. Finish and serve: Sprinkle with Parmesan cheese if desired and garnish with fresh basil leaves. Serve immediately.

Nutritional Values (per serving):

- Calories: 180
- Fat: 8g
- Carbohydrates: 25g
- Protein: 5g

Grilled Chicken with Mango Salsa and Brown Rice

Ingredients:

- 2 boneless, skinless chicken breasts
- 1 tablespoon olive oil
- 1 teaspoon cumin
- 1/2 teaspoon chili powder
- Salt and pepper to taste
- 1 cup cooked brown rice
- For the Mango Salsa:
- 1 ripe mango, diced
- 1/4 cup red bell pepper, diced
- 1/4 cup red onion, finely chopped
- 1 tablespoon fresh cilantro, chopped
- 1 tablespoon lime juice
- Salt to taste

Directions:

1. Prepare the chicken: Rub the chicken breasts with olive oil, cumin, chili powder, salt, and pepper. Let marinate for 15-20 minutes while you prepare the mango salsa.
2. Make the mango salsa: In a medium bowl, combine the diced

mango, red bell pepper, red onion, cilantro, lime juice, and a pinch of salt. Mix well and set aside.

3. Cook the chicken: Heat a grill or grill pan over medium-high heat. Grill the chicken for 6-7 minutes on each side, or until fully cooked and the internal temperature reaches 165°F (74°C). Remove from the grill and let rest for a few minutes before slicing.
4. Assemble the dish: Divide the cooked brown rice among plates. Top each serving with sliced grilled chicken and a generous scoop of mango salsa.
5. Serve: Garnish with additional cilantro or a wedge of lime if desired. Serve warm and enjoy the combination of sweet, spicy, and savory flavors.

Nutritional Values (per serving):

- Calories: 380
- Fat: 10g
- Carbohydrates: 42g
- Protein: 32g

Coconut-Lime Grilled Fish Tacos

Ingredients:

- 1 pound white fish fillets (such as cod, mahi-mahi, or tilapia)
- 1/4 cup coconut milk
- Juice and zest of 1 lime
- 1 teaspoon chili powder
- 1/2 teaspoon garlic powder
- Salt and pepper to taste
- 8 small corn or flour tortillas
- 1 cup shredded red cabbage
- 1/2 cup diced pineapple (optional, for sweetness)
- 1/4 cup fresh cilantro, chopped
- For the Sauce:
- 1/4 cup plain Greek yogurt
- 1 tablespoon lime juice
- 1 teaspoon honey or agave syrup
- Salt to taste

Directions:

1. Marinate the fish: In a shallow dish, whisk together the coconut milk, lime juice and zest, chili powder, garlic powder, salt, and pepper. Add the fish fillets, ensuring they are fully coated. Cover and refrigerate for 20-30 minutes to marinate.
2. Prepare the sauce: In a small bowl, combine the Greek yogurt, lime juice, honey, and a pinch of salt. Mix until smooth and set aside.
3. Grill the fish: Preheat a grill or grill pan over medium heat. Remove the fish from the marinade and grill for 3-4 minutes per side, or until the fish is opaque and flakes easily with a fork. Set aside to cool slightly, then flake into bite-sized pieces.
4. Warm the tortillas: Heat the tortillas in a dry skillet or on the grill for about 30 seconds per side, until warm and pliable.

5. Assemble the tacos: Fill each tortilla with a portion of grilled fish. Top with shredded red cabbage, diced pineapple (if using), and a drizzle of the prepared sauce. Garnish with fresh cilantro.
6. Serve immediately: Enjoy your tacos with a squeeze of lime for extra flavor.

Nutritional Values (per serving):

- Calories: 300
- Fat: 10g
- Carbohydrates: 28g
- Protein: 25g

Baked Salmon with Broccoli and Lemon

Ingredients:

- 2 salmon fillets (about 6 ounces each)
- 2 cups broccoli florets
- 1 tablespoon olive oil
- 2 cloves garlic, minced
- Juice and zest of 1 lemon
- 1/2 teaspoon dried thyme
- Salt and pepper to taste
- Lemon wedges for serving

Directions:

1. Preheat the oven to 400°F (200°C). Line a baking sheet with parchment paper or lightly grease it with olive oil.
2. Prepare the broccoli: Toss the broccoli florets with half of the olive oil, minced garlic, salt, and pepper. Spread them on one side of the baking sheet.
3. Season the salmon: Place the salmon fillets on the other side of the baking sheet. Drizzle them with the remaining olive oil, sprinkle with dried thyme, and season with salt and pepper. Squeeze half of the lemon juice over the salmon and broccoli.
4. Bake: Place the baking sheet in the preheated oven and bake for 12-15 minutes, or until the salmon is opaque and flakes easily with a fork and the broccoli is tender with slightly crispy edges.
5. Garnish and serve: Remove from the oven and sprinkle the salmon with lemon zest. Serve immediately with lemon wedges on the side for an extra burst of flavor.

Nutritional Values (per serving):

- Calories: 320
- Fat: 20g
- Carbohydrates: 8g
- Protein: 28g

Spicy Turkey Meatballs with Cauliflower Rice

Ingredients:
For the Meatballs:

- 1 pound ground turkey
- 1/4 cup breadcrumbs (or almond flour for a low-carb option)

- 1 egg, beaten
- 2 cloves garlic, minced
- 1 teaspoon smoked paprika
- 1 teaspoon chili powder (adjust to taste)
- 1/2 teaspoon cumin
- Salt and pepper to taste
- 1 tablespoon olive oil (for cooking)

For the Cauliflower Rice:

- 1 medium head of cauliflower, grated or processed into rice-sized pieces
- 1 tablespoon olive oil
- 1 small onion, diced
- 1 clove garlic, minced
- Salt and pepper to taste
- Optional: chopped fresh parsley or cilantro for garnish

Directions:

1. Prepare the meatball mixture: In a large bowl, combine the ground turkey, breadcrumbs, egg, minced garlic, smoked paprika, chili powder, cumin, salt, and pepper. Mix until well combined.
2. Form the meatballs: Roll the mixture into small, evenly-sized balls (about 1-1.5 inches in diameter).
3. Cook the meatballs: Heat the olive oil in a large skillet over medium heat. Add the meatballs and cook for 8-10 minutes, turning occasionally, until they are browned on all sides and cooked through. Remove from the skillet and set aside.
4. Prepare the cauliflower rice: In the same skillet, heat the olive oil over medium heat. Add the diced onion and garlic, sautéing until softened and fragrant, about 3-4 minutes. Add the grated cauliflower and cook for another 5-7 minutes, stirring frequently, until tender. Season with salt and pepper to taste.
5. Serve: Plate the cauliflower rice and top with the spicy turkey meatballs. Garnish with fresh parsley or cilantro if desired.

Nutritional Values (per serving):

- Calories: 320
- Fat: 15g
- Carbohydrates: 12g
- Protein: 34g

Miso-Glazed Salmon with Cucumber Salad

Ingredients:
For the Salmon:

- 2 salmon fillets (about 6 ounces each)
- 2 tablespoons white miso paste
- 1 tablespoon honey or maple syrup
- 1 tablespoon rice vinegar
- 1 teaspoon soy sauce
- 1 teaspoon sesame oil

For the Cucumber Salad:

- 1 large cucumber, thinly sliced

- 1/4 cup rice vinegar
- 1 teaspoon sesame oil
- 1 teaspoon honey or sugar (optional, for sweetness)
- 1 tablespoon sesame seeds
- Salt to taste

Directions:

1. Prepare the miso glaze: In a small bowl, whisk together the miso paste, honey or maple syrup, rice vinegar, soy sauce, and sesame oil until smooth.
2. Glaze the salmon: Place the salmon fillets on a lined baking sheet, skin-side down. Brush the miso glaze generously over the top of the fillets. Let them marinate for 10-15 minutes while you prepare the cucumber salad.
3. Make the cucumber salad: In a mixing bowl, combine the sliced cucumber, rice vinegar, sesame oil, honey or sugar (if using), sesame seeds, and a pinch of salt. Toss well to coat the cucumbers evenly. Set aside to let the flavors meld.
4. Cook the salmon: Preheat your oven's broiler on high. Place the salmon under the broiler and cook for 6-8 minutes, or until the glaze is caramelized and the salmon is cooked through. Watch carefully to prevent burning.
5. Serve: Plate the miso-glazed salmon alongside a portion of cucumber salad. Garnish with additional sesame seeds or chopped green onions if desired.

Nutritional Values (per serving):

- Calories: 330
- Fat: 18g
- Carbohydrates: 12g
- Protein: 30g

Eggplant & Lentil Stew with Garlic Bread

Ingredients:
For the Stew:

- 1 medium eggplant, diced
- 1 cup cooked lentils (green or brown)
- 1 can (14 oz) diced tomatoes
- 1 small onion, chopped
- 2 cloves garlic, minced
- 2 tablespoons olive oil
- 1 teaspoon smoked paprika
- 1 teaspoon cumin
- 1/2 teaspoon chili powder (optional, for heat)
- 2 cups vegetable broth
- Salt and pepper to taste
- Fresh parsley or cilantro for garnish

For the Garlic Bread:

- 4 slices of whole-grain or sourdough bread
- 2 tablespoons butter or olive oil
- 1 clove garlic, minced
- 1 tablespoon fresh parsley, chopped

Directions:

1. Prepare the stew: Heat the olive oil in a large pot over medium heat. Add the onion and garlic, sautéing until softened, about 3-4 minutes.
2. Cook the eggplant: Add the diced eggplant to the pot and cook for 5-7 minutes, stirring occasionally, until it begins to soften and lightly brown.
3. Add spices and broth: Stir in the smoked paprika, cumin, and chili powder (if using). Add the diced tomatoes, vegetable broth, and lentils. Season with salt and pepper to taste.
4. Simmer the stew: Reduce the heat to low and let the stew simmer for 20-25 minutes, stirring occasionally, until the eggplant is tender and the flavors are well combined.
5. Make the garlic bread: While the stew is simmering, preheat your oven to 375°F (190°C). In a small bowl, mix the butter or olive oil with the minced garlic and chopped parsley. Spread this mixture evenly over the bread slices. Place the bread on a baking sheet and bake for 8-10 minutes, or until golden and crispy.
6. Serve: Ladle the eggplant and lentil stew into bowls and serve with a slice of warm garlic bread on the side. Garnish the stew with fresh parsley or cilantro for added flavor.

Nutritional Values (per serving):

- Calories: 380
- Fat: 12g
- Carbohydrates: 52g
- Protein: 14g

Garlic Butter Shrimp with Zoodles

Ingredients:

- 1 pound shrimp, peeled and deveined
- 4 medium zucchinis, spiralized into noodles
- 3 tablespoons butter
- 3 cloves garlic, minced
- 1/4 teaspoon red pepper flakes (optional, for heat)
- Juice of 1 lemon
- 2 tablespoons fresh parsley, chopped
- Salt and pepper to taste

Directions:

1. Prepare the shrimp: Pat the shrimp dry with a paper towel and season lightly with salt and pepper.
2. Cook the shrimp: Heat 2 tablespoons of butter in a large skillet over medium heat. Add the minced garlic and red pepper flakes (if using) and sauté for about 30 seconds until fragrant. Add the shrimp and cook for 2-3 minutes per side, or until they turn pink and opaque. Remove the

shrimp from the skillet and set aside.
3. Cook the zoodles: In the same skillet, add the remaining tablespoon of butter. Add the zucchini noodles and toss gently to coat in the garlic butter. Cook for 2-3 minutes, stirring occasionally, until the zoodles are just tender but still crisp. Avoid overcooking to prevent them from becoming soggy.
4. Combine and finish: Return the cooked shrimp to the skillet with the zoodles. Drizzle with lemon juice and toss gently to combine. Adjust seasoning with more salt and pepper if needed.
5. Serve: Divide the garlic butter shrimp and zoodles among plates. Garnish with fresh parsley and serve immediately.

Nutritional Values (per serving):

- Calories: 250
- Fat: 15g
- Carbohydrates: 6g
- Protein: 25g

Sweet Potato & Kale Buddha Bowl

Ingredients:

- 1 large sweet potato, peeled and cubed
- 2 cups kale, chopped (stems removed)
- 1 cup cooked quinoa
- 1/2 cup canned chickpeas, rinsed and drained
- 1 tablespoon olive oil
- 1 teaspoon smoked paprika
- 1/2 teaspoon garlic powder
- Salt and pepper to taste
- 1 tablespoon tahini
- 1 tablespoon lemon juice
- 1 teaspoon maple syrup or honey
- Optional: sesame seeds or sliced avocado for garnish

Directions:

1. Roast the sweet potatoes: Preheat your oven to 400°F (200°C). Toss the sweet potato cubes with 1/2 tablespoon of olive oil, smoked paprika, garlic powder, salt, and pepper. Spread them on a baking sheet in a single layer and roast for 20-25 minutes, flipping halfway through, until tender and slightly caramelized.
2. Prepare the kale: While the sweet potatoes are roasting, heat the remaining 1/2 tablespoon of olive oil in a skillet over medium heat. Add the chopped kale, season with salt and pepper, and sauté for 3-4 minutes until wilted. Remove from heat and set aside.
3. Prepare the dressing: In a small bowl, whisk together the tahini, lemon juice, and maple syrup or honey. Add a splash of water to thin the dressing if needed.

4. Assemble the bowl: Divide the cooked quinoa among serving bowls. Top each bowl with roasted sweet potatoes, sautéed kale, and chickpeas. Drizzle the tahini dressing over the top.
5. Garnish and serve: Sprinkle with sesame seeds or add sliced avocado if desired. Serve warm or at room temperature.

Nutritional Values (per serving):

- Calories: 360
- Fat: 12g
- Carbohydrates: 55g
- Protein: 12g

Grilled Tempeh with Brussels Sprouts

Ingredients:

- 1 block (8 oz) tempeh, sliced into thin strips
- 2 cups Brussels sprouts, halved
- 2 tablespoons olive oil
- 2 tablespoons soy sauce or tamari (for gluten-free)
- 1 tablespoon balsamic vinegar
- 1 teaspoon garlic powder
- 1/2 teaspoon smoked paprika
- Salt and pepper to taste
- Optional: fresh parsley for garnish

Directions:

1. Marinate the tempeh: In a shallow dish, mix 1 tablespoon olive oil, soy sauce, balsamic vinegar, garlic powder, smoked paprika, salt, and pepper. Add the tempeh slices to the marinade, turning to coat them evenly. Let marinate for at least 15 minutes while you prepare the Brussels sprouts.
2. Prepare the Brussels sprouts: Toss the halved Brussels sprouts with the remaining olive oil, salt, and pepper. Preheat your grill or grill pan to medium heat.
3. Grill the tempeh: Remove the tempeh from the marinade and place it on the grill. Cook for about 3-4 minutes per side, or until golden and lightly charred.
4. Grill the Brussels sprouts: Place the Brussels sprouts on the grill or a grilling tray. Cook for 4-5 minutes per side, turning occasionally, until tender and slightly caramelized.
5. Serve: Arrange the grilled tempeh and Brussels sprouts on a plate. Drizzle any remaining marinade over the tempeh for extra flavor and garnish with fresh parsley if desired.

Nutritional Values (per serving):

- Calories: 280
- Fat: 14g
- Carbohydrates: 20g
- Protein: 20g

Roasted Veggie & Quinoa Stir-Fry

Ingredients:

- 1 cup cooked quinoa

- 2 cups mixed vegetables (such as zucchini, bell peppers, broccoli, and carrots), chopped
- 2 tablespoons olive oil
- 2 cloves garlic, minced
- 1 tablespoon soy sauce or tamari (for gluten-free)
- 1 teaspoon sesame oil
- 1/2 teaspoon smoked paprika
- Salt and pepper to taste
- Optional toppings: sesame seeds, green onions

Directions:

1. Roast the vegetables: Preheat your oven to 400°F (200°C). Toss the mixed vegetables with 1 tablespoon of olive oil, smoked paprika, salt, and pepper. Spread them out on a baking sheet and roast for 20-25 minutes, turning halfway through, until tender and slightly caramelized.
2. Cook the quinoa: If not already prepared, cook the quinoa according to package instructions. Typically, rinse 1 cup of quinoa and cook in 2 cups of water for about 15 minutes, or until tender and the water is absorbed.
3. Sauté garlic: Heat the remaining 1 tablespoon of olive oil in a large skillet over medium heat. Add the minced garlic and sauté for about 1 minute, until fragrant.
4. Combine and stir-fry: Add the roasted vegetables to the skillet along with the cooked quinoa. Drizzle with soy sauce and sesame oil, tossing well to coat evenly. Stir-fry for 2-3 minutes to heat everything through.
5. Serve: Divide the stir-fry into bowls and garnish with optional toppings like sesame seeds or sliced green onions. Serve hot.

Nutritional Values (per serving):

- Calories: 290
- Fat: 12g
- Carbohydrates: 35g
- Protein: 8g

Lemon Garlic Chicken with Sautéed Spinach

Ingredients:

- 2 boneless, skinless chicken breasts
- 3 tablespoons olive oil, divided
- 2 cloves garlic, minced
- Juice and zest of 1 lemon
- 1 teaspoon dried oregano
- Salt and pepper to taste
- 4 cups fresh spinach leaves

Directions:

1. Prepare the chicken: Pat the chicken breasts dry and season both sides with salt, pepper, and dried oregano.
2. Cook the chicken: Heat 2 tablespoons of olive oil in a large

skillet over medium-high heat. Add the chicken breasts and cook for 5-7 minutes on each side, or until golden brown and cooked through with an internal temperature of 165°F (74°C). Remove the chicken from the skillet and set aside to rest.

3. Make the lemon garlic sauce: In the same skillet, lower the heat to medium. Add the remaining 1 tablespoon of olive oil and the minced garlic. Sauté for 1 minute, being careful not to burn the garlic. Add the lemon juice and zest, stirring to deglaze the pan and create a light sauce.
4. Sauté the spinach: Add the fresh spinach to the skillet and toss it in the lemon garlic sauce. Cook for 2-3 minutes, stirring occasionally, until the spinach is wilted but still vibrant.
5. Serve: Plate the sautéed spinach and top with the cooked chicken breasts. Drizzle any remaining lemon garlic sauce over the chicken and serve immediately.

Nutritional Values (per serving):

- Calories: 320
- Fat: 18g
- Carbohydrates: 5g
- Protein: 35g

Salmon & Avocado Wraps

Ingredients:

- 2 large whole-grain tortillas or wraps
- 4 ounces cooked salmon, flaked
- 1 ripe avocado, sliced
- 1 cup mixed greens (such as spinach, arugula, or lettuce)
- 1/4 cup cucumber, thinly sliced
- 2 tablespoons plain Greek yogurt
- 1 teaspoon lemon juice
- Salt and pepper to taste

Directions:

1. Prepare the spread: In a small bowl, mix the Greek yogurt with lemon juice, and season with a pinch of salt and pepper.
2. Assemble the wraps: Lay each tortilla flat and spread a layer of the prepared yogurt mixture across the surface.
3. Add the fillings: Arrange the mixed greens, flaked salmon, avocado slices, and cucumber evenly in the center of each tortilla.
4. Wrap tightly: Fold in the sides of the tortilla and roll it tightly into a wrap. Slice in half for easier serving if desired.
5. Serve immediately: Enjoy the wraps fresh, or wrap them in foil or parchment paper for an easy, on-the-go meal.

Nutritional Values (per serving):

- Calories: 340
- Fat: 18g
- Carbohydrates: 22g
- Protein: 22g

Grilled Steak with Roasted Vegetables

Ingredients:

- 2 steaks (such as sirloin or ribeye, about 6-8 ounces each)
- 2 tablespoons olive oil, divided
- 1 teaspoon garlic powder
- 1 teaspoon dried rosemary or thyme
- Salt and pepper to taste
- 1 cup broccoli florets
- 1 cup diced zucchini
- 1 cup diced bell peppers (red, yellow, or green)
- 1 medium carrot, sliced

Directions:

1. Prepare the vegetables: Preheat your oven to 400°F (200°C). In a mixing bowl, toss the broccoli, zucchini, bell peppers, and carrot with 1 tablespoon olive oil, garlic powder, salt, and pepper. Spread the vegetables evenly on a baking sheet.
2. Roast the vegetables: Place the baking sheet in the preheated oven and roast for 20-25 minutes, stirring halfway through, until the vegetables are tender and slightly caramelized.
3. Prepare the steaks: While the vegetables are roasting, season the steaks with salt, pepper, and dried rosemary or thyme. Drizzle with the remaining olive oil.
4. Grill the steaks: Preheat a grill or grill pan over medium-high heat. Cook the steaks for 4-5 minutes per side for medium-rare, or until they reach your desired doneness. Use a meat thermometer for accuracy (130°F for medium-rare, 140°F for medium). Let the steaks rest for 5 minutes before slicing.
5. Serve: Arrange the roasted vegetables on plates and place the grilled steak on top or alongside. Serve immediately.

Nutritional Values (per serving):

- Calories: 450
- Fat: 25g
- Carbohydrates: 20g
- Protein: 40g

Sweet Potato & Black Bean Tacos

Ingredients:

- 2 medium sweet potatoes, peeled and diced
- 1 tablespoon olive oil
- 1 teaspoon smoked paprika
- 1/2 teaspoon cumin
- Salt and pepper to taste
- 1 can (15 oz) black beans, rinsed and drained
- 8 small corn or flour tortillas
- 1/2 cup red cabbage, shredded

- 1/4 cup fresh cilantro, chopped
- Optional toppings: avocado slices, salsa, lime wedges, or Greek yogurt

Directions:

1. Roast the sweet potatoes: Preheat your oven to 400°F (200°C). Toss the diced sweet potatoes with olive oil, smoked paprika, cumin, salt, and pepper. Spread them in a single layer on a baking sheet and roast for 20-25 minutes, flipping halfway through, until tender and slightly caramelized.
2. Warm the black beans: In a small saucepan over low heat, warm the black beans. Season with a pinch of salt and pepper if desired.
3. Prepare the tortillas: Heat the tortillas in a dry skillet or over a flame for about 30 seconds per side, or until warm and pliable.
4. Assemble the tacos: Divide the roasted sweet potatoes and black beans evenly among the tortillas. Top with shredded red cabbage, fresh cilantro, and any additional toppings you like, such as avocado slices, salsa, lime wedges, or a dollop of Greek yogurt.
- Serve: Enjoy the tacos fresh with a squeeze of lime juice for added brightness.
- **Nutritional Values (per serving):**
- Calories: 300
- Fat: 8g
- Carbohydrates: 45g
- Protein: 10g

Lemon Herb Chicken with Roasted Sweet Potatoes

Ingredients:
For the Chicken:

- 2 boneless, skinless chicken breasts
- 2 tablespoons olive oil
- Juice and zest of 1 lemon
- 1 teaspoon dried oregano
- 1 teaspoon garlic powder
- Salt and pepper to taste
- For the Sweet Potatoes:
- 2 medium sweet potatoes, peeled and cubed
- 1 tablespoon olive oil
- 1/2 teaspoon smoked paprika
- 1/2 teaspoon cumin
- Salt and pepper to taste

Directions:

1. Preheat the oven to 400°F (200°C).
2. Prepare the sweet potatoes: Toss the sweet potato cubes with olive oil, smoked paprika, cumin, salt, and pepper. Spread them in a single layer on a baking sheet. Roast in the oven for 25-30 minutes, flipping halfway through, until tender and slightly caramelized.
3. Marinate the chicken: In a small bowl, mix olive oil, lemon juice

and zest, oregano, garlic powder, salt, and pepper. Pour the mixture over the chicken breasts and let them marinate for at least 15 minutes while the sweet potatoes roast.

4. Cook the chicken: Heat a grill pan or skillet over medium-high heat. Remove the chicken from the marinade and cook for 5-7 minutes per side, or until fully cooked with an internal temperature of 165°F (74°C). Remove from heat and let the chicken rest for 5 minutes before slicing.
5. Serve: Plate the roasted sweet potatoes alongside the sliced lemon herb chicken. Garnish with additional lemon zest or fresh herbs if desired.

Nutritional Values (per serving):

- Calories: 420
- Fat: 16g
- Carbohydrates: 30g
- Protein: 38g

Teriyaki Salmon with Veggie Stir-Fry

Ingredients:
For the Salmon:

- 2 salmon fillets (about 6 ounces each)
- 1/4 cup teriyaki sauce (store-bought or homemade)
- For the Veggie Stir-Fry:
- 1 tablespoon olive oil
- 1 cup broccoli florets
- 1 red bell pepper, sliced
- 1 carrot, julienned
- 1 zucchini, sliced
- 2 cloves garlic, minced
- 2 tablespoons soy sauce or tamari (for gluten-free)
- 1 teaspoon sesame oil
- Optional: sesame seeds and sliced green onions for garnish

Directions:

1. Marinate the salmon: Place the salmon fillets in a shallow dish and pour the teriyaki sauce over them. Let marinate for 15-20 minutes while you prepare the vegetables.
2. Cook the salmon: Preheat a skillet or grill pan over medium-high heat. Remove the salmon from the marinade and cook for 3-4 minutes per side, or until the salmon is cooked through and caramelized. Set aside and keep warm.
3. Prepare the stir-fry: Heat olive oil in a large skillet or wok over medium-high heat. Add the broccoli, red bell pepper, carrot, and zucchini. Stir-fry for 4-5 minutes, or until the vegetables are tender but still crisp.
4. Add the flavoring: Stir in the garlic, soy sauce, and sesame oil. Toss well to coat the vegetables evenly and cook for another 1-2 minutes.
5. Serve: Divide the veggie stir-fry among plates and top with the

teriyaki salmon. Garnish with sesame seeds and sliced green onions if desired.

Nutritional Values (per serving):

- Calories: 380
- Fat: 18g
- Carbohydrates: 18g
- Protein: 38g

Snacks

Snacks can be a delightful and essential part of any day, providing that perfect boost between meals. This collection of 25 snack recipes is designed to cater to a variety of tastes and dietary needs, ensuring you find just the right treat to satisfy your cravings while supporting your wellness goals. Whether you're in need of a quick energy boost, a portable option for on-the-go, or a cozy treat to enjoy with a warm drink, these recipes offer nutritious, easy-to-prepare solutions to keep you energized and satisfied.

Avocado & Hummus Toast

Ingredients:

- 2 slices of whole grain bread
- 1 ripe avocado
- 1/4 cup hummus
- Salt and pepper to taste
- Optional toppings: cherry tomatoes, arugula, red pepper flakes

Directions:

1. Toast the bread: Begin by toasting the bread slices to your desired crispness.
2. Prepare the avocado: While the bread is toasting, halve the avocado and remove the pit. Scoop the avocado flesh into a bowl, mash it with a fork, and season with salt and pepper.
3. Spread the hummus: Once the bread is toasted, spread each slice evenly with hummus.
4. Add the mashed avocado: Spoon the mashed avocado over the hummus layer on each slice of toast.
5. Add toppings: If using, add optional toppings like sliced cherry tomatoes, arugula, or a sprinkle of red pepper flakes for extra flavor.
6. Serve immediately: Enjoy your Avocado & Hummus Toast fresh for the best texture and taste.

Nutritional Values (per serving):

- Calories: 290
- Fat: 20g
- Carbohydrates: 22g
- Protein: 12g

Protein-Packed Energy Balls

Ingredients:

- 1 cup rolled oats
- 1/2 cup natural peanut butter (or any nut butter of choice)
- 1/4 cup honey or maple syrup
- 1/4 cup protein powder (your choice of flavor)
- 1/4 cup mini chocolate chips or dried fruit (such as cranberries or raisins)

- 2 tablespoons chia seeds
- 2 tablespoons flaxseeds
- 1 teaspoon vanilla extract
- A pinch of salt

Directions:

1. Mix the ingredients: In a large mixing bowl, combine the rolled oats, peanut butter, honey or maple syrup, protein powder, chocolate chips or dried fruit, chia seeds, flaxseeds, vanilla extract, and a pinch of salt. Stir until all ingredients are well mixed and the mixture is sticky.
2. Form the balls: Wet your hands slightly (this helps prevent sticking) and take small portions of the mixture to roll into balls, about 1 inch in diameter.
3. Chill the balls: Place the energy balls on a baking sheet lined with parchment paper. Refrigerate for at least 30 minutes to set, which helps them hold their shape better.
4. Store: Keep the energy balls in an airtight container in the refrigerator for up to a week or freeze for longer storage.
5. Serve: Enjoy these energy balls as a quick snack, a pre-workout boost, or a sweet treat after meals.

Nutritional Values (per serving, approximately 2 balls):

- Calories: 180
- Fat: 10g
- Carbohydrates: 20g
- Protein: 7g

Chia & Coconut Protein Bars

Ingredients:

- 1 cup rolled oats
- 1/2 cup protein powder (vanilla or unflavored)
- 1/4 cup chia seeds
- 1/2 cup shredded unsweetened coconut
- 1/2 cup almond butter (or any nut butter of your choice)
- 1/3 cup honey or maple syrup
- 1/4 cup coconut oil, melted
- 1 teaspoon vanilla extract
- Pinch of salt

Directions:

1. Prepare the mixture: In a large mixing bowl, combine the rolled oats, protein powder, chia seeds, and shredded coconut. Mix thoroughly to blend the dry ingredients.
2. Combine the wet ingredients: In a separate bowl, whisk together the almond butter, honey or maple syrup, melted coconut oil, vanilla extract, and a pinch of salt until smooth.
3. Mix together: Pour the wet ingredients over the dry ingredients and stir until everything is thoroughly combined and the mixture is sticky and uniform.

4. Press into a pan: Line an 8x8 inch baking pan with parchment paper, allowing some overhang for easy removal. Transfer the mixture to the pan and press down firmly into an even layer.
5. Chill to set: Refrigerate the mixture for at least 2-3 hours, or until firm. This helps the bars to set and makes them easier to cut.
6. Cut into bars: Once chilled and firm, lift the mixture out of the pan using the overhanging parchment paper. Place on a cutting board and slice into bars or squares.
7. Store: Keep the protein bars in an airtight container in the refrigerator for up to a week or freeze for longer storage.
8. Serve: Enjoy these Chia & Coconut Protein Bars as a nutritious snack, perfect for a post-workout recovery or a midday energy boost.

Nutritional Values (per bar, if cut into 12 bars):

- Calories: 220
- Fat: 12g
- Carbohydrates: 20g
- Protein: 8g

Baked Sweet Potato Fries

Ingredients:

- 2 large sweet potatoes, peeled and cut into 1/4-inch thick sticks
- 2 tablespoons olive oil
- 1 teaspoon paprika
- 1/2 teaspoon garlic powder
- Salt and pepper to taste
- Optional: fresh parsley, chopped for garnish

Directions:

1. Preheat the oven: Set your oven to 425°F (220°C). Line a baking sheet with parchment paper for easy cleanup.
2. Season the fries: In a large bowl, toss the sweet potato sticks with olive oil, paprika, garlic powder, salt, and pepper until they are evenly coated.
3. Arrange on baking sheet: Spread the sweet potato fries in a single layer on the prepared baking sheet, making sure they don't overlap to ensure even cooking.
4. Bake: Place the baking sheet in the preheated oven and bake for 20-25 minutes, turning the fries halfway through the cooking time, until they are golden and crisp.
5. Garnish and serve: Once baked, remove the fries from the oven and, if desired, sprinkle with chopped fresh parsley for added flavor and color. Serve hot, ideally with your favorite dipping sauce.

Nutritional Values (per serving):

- Calories: 200
- Fat: 7g
- Carbohydrates: 32g

- Protein: 2g

Greek Yogurt & Berry Parfait

Ingredients:

- 1 cup Greek yogurt (plain or vanilla)
- 1/2 cup mixed berries (such as strawberries, blueberries, and raspberries)
- 1/4 cup granola
- 1 tablespoon honey or maple syrup (optional)
- Optional garnishes: a sprinkle of chia seeds or a drizzle of honey

Directions:

1. Prepare the berries: If using strawberries, hull and slice them. Rinse other berries and pat dry to ensure they mix well without extra moisture.
2. Layer the parfait: In a serving glass or bowl, start with a layer of Greek yogurt. Add a layer of mixed berries on top of the yogurt.
3. Add granola: Sprinkle a layer of granola over the berries for a crunchy texture.
4. Repeat layers: Continue layering yogurt, berries, and granola until the glass is filled to your liking. Typically, two layers of each component create a balanced parfait.
5. Top and serve: Drizzle honey or maple syrup over the top for added sweetness if desired. Garnish with chia seeds or an extra drizzle of honey.
6. Serve immediately: Enjoy this Greek Yogurt & Berry Parfait as a fresh and healthy snack, perfect for breakfast or as a delightful dessert.

Nutritional Values (per serving):

- Calories: 280
- Fat: 4g
- Carbohydrates: 42g
- Protein: 20g

Carrot Sticks with Almond Butter

Ingredients:

- 4 large carrots, peeled and cut into sticks
- 1/2 cup almond butter
- Optional toppings: a sprinkle of sea salt or cinnamon

Directions:

1. Prepare the carrots: Wash, peel, and cut the carrots into stick-shaped pieces, about 3 to 4 inches long and 1/2 inch thick.
2. Serve with almond butter: Place the almond butter in a small serving bowl. If the almond butter is too thick, you can stir in a little warm water or coconut oil to make it more dip-like in consistency.
3. Add optional toppings: Sprinkle the almond butter with a pinch of sea salt or a dash of cinnamon to enhance the flavor, if desired.

4. **Arrange and enjoy:** Arrange the carrot sticks around the bowl of almond butter for easy dipping. Serve as a healthy snack or appetizer.

Nutritional Values (per serving):

- Calories: 280 (including 1/4 cup of almond butter per serving)
- Fat: 18g
- Carbohydrates: 20g
- Protein: 8g

Roasted Chickpeas with Turmeric

Ingredients:

- 1 can (15 oz) chickpeas, drained, rinsed, and patted dry
- 2 tablespoons olive oil
- 1 teaspoon turmeric
- 1/2 teaspoon garlic powder
- 1/2 teaspoon paprika
- Salt and pepper to taste

Directions:

1. **Preheat the oven:** Set your oven to 400°F (200°C). Line a baking sheet with parchment paper for easy cleanup.
2. **Season the chickpeas:** In a bowl, toss the dried chickpeas with olive oil, turmeric, garlic powder, paprika, salt, and pepper until evenly coated.
3. **Bake the chickpeas:** Spread the seasoned chickpeas in a single layer on the prepared baking sheet. Bake in the preheated oven for 20-30 minutes, stirring occasionally, until they are golden and crispy.
4. **Cool and serve:** Remove the chickpeas from the oven and let them cool on the baking sheet for a few minutes; they will continue to crisp up as they cool. Serve warm or at room temperature as a snack.

Nutritional Values (per serving):

- Calories: 150
- Fat: 8g
- Carbohydrates: 15g
- Protein: 5g

Apple with Almond Butter & Cinnamon

Ingredients:

- 1 large apple, cored and sliced
- 1/4 cup almond butter
- 1/2 teaspoon ground cinnamon
- Optional: a drizzle of honey or a sprinkle of granola for added texture

Directions:

1. **Prepare the apple:** Wash the apple thoroughly, remove the core, and slice it into even wedges.
2. **Serve with almond butter:** Place the almond butter in a small serving bowl. Stir in the ground cinnamon until well combined. If you prefer a sweeter taste, you can mix a drizzle of honey into the almond butter.

3. **Arrange and enjoy:** Arrange the apple slices on a plate around the bowl of almond butter. Sprinkle additional cinnamon over the apple slices for extra flavor, and if desired, add a sprinkle of granola for crunch.
4. **Serve immediately:** Enjoy dipping the apple slices into the spiced almond butter. This snack is not only delicious but also offers a good mix of natural sugars, healthy fats, and protein.

Nutritional Values (per serving):

- Calories: 280
- Fat: 18g
- Carbohydrates: 25g
- Protein: 8g

Celery & Peanut Butter Sticks

Ingredients:

- 5 stalks of celery, washed and trimmed
- 1/2 cup smooth or crunchy peanut butter
- Optional toppings: raisins, dried cranberries, or chopped nuts

Directions:

1. **Prepare the celery:** Cut the celery stalks into 3 to 4-inch pieces. Ensure they are thoroughly cleaned and dried.
2. **Fill with peanut butter:** Using a small spoon or a knife, fill the concave side of each celery stick with peanut butter. Spread evenly along the length of the celery.
3. **Add toppings:** If desired, sprinkle optional toppings such as raisins, dried cranberries, or chopped nuts over the peanut butter for additional flavor and texture.
4. **Chill and serve:** For an extra crisp snack, you can chill the prepared celery sticks in the refrigerator for about 30 minutes before serving. This step is optional but can enhance the texture and make the peanut butter slightly more firm.

Nutritional Values (per serving):

- Calories: 160
- Fat: 12g
- Carbohydrates: 8g
- Protein: 6g

Coconut & Cashew Energy Bites

Ingredients:

- 1 cup cashews
- 1/2 cup shredded unsweetened coconut, plus extra for rolling
- 1/2 cup pitted dates
- 1 teaspoon vanilla extract
- 1/4 teaspoon salt
- 2 tablespoons coconut oil

Directions:

1. **Process the mixture:** In a food processor, combine the cashews, half of the shredded coconut, dates, vanilla extract, salt, and coconut oil. Process until the mixture is

finely chopped and sticks together when pressed between your fingers.
2. Form the bites: Scoop out the mixture by the tablespoon and roll into balls. If the mixture is too dry to form balls, you can add a little more coconut oil or a splash of water to help it stick together.
3. Coat with coconut: Place the remaining shredded coconut in a shallow dish. Roll each ball in the coconut to coat thoroughly.
4. Chill to set: Place the energy bites on a baking sheet or plate lined with parchment paper. Refrigerate for at least 30 minutes to allow the bites to firm up.
5. Store: Keep the coconut & cashew energy bites in an airtight container in the refrigerator for up to a week or in the freezer for longer storage.
6. Serve: Enjoy these energy bites as a quick snack, perfect for a pre-workout boost or a midday energy lift.

Nutritional Values (per bite, if making 12 bites):

- Calories: 150
- Fat: 10g
- Carbohydrates: 13g
- Protein: 3g

Spicy Roasted Pumpkin Seeds

Ingredients:

- 1 cup raw pumpkin seeds, cleaned and dried
- 1 tablespoon olive oil
- 1/2 teaspoon chili powder
- 1/4 teaspoon cayenne pepper (adjust based on heat preference)
- 1/2 teaspoon garlic powder
- Salt to taste

Directions:

1. Preheat the oven: Set your oven to 300°F (150°C). Line a baking sheet with parchment paper for easy cleanup.
2. Season the seeds: In a bowl, toss the pumpkin seeds with olive oil, chili powder, cayenne pepper, garlic powder, and salt until they are evenly coated.
3. Roast the seeds: Spread the seasoned pumpkin seeds in a single layer on the prepared baking sheet. Roast in the preheated oven for about 45 minutes, stirring occasionally, until they are golden and crispy.
4. Cool and serve: Remove the seeds from the oven and allow them to cool on the baking sheet. The seeds will continue to crisp up as they cool.
5. Store: Once cooled, store the spicy roasted pumpkin seeds in an airtight container at room temperature for up to 2 weeks.

Nutritional Values (per serving, about 1/4 cup):

- Calories: 180
- Fat: 15g
- Carbohydrates: 3g
- Protein: 9g

Cucumber & Cream Cheese Bites

Ingredients:

- 1 large English cucumber
- 1/2 cup cream cheese, softened
- 1 tablespoon fresh dill, chopped
- 1 teaspoon lemon zest
- Salt and pepper to taste
- Optional garnishes: smoked salmon, dill sprigs, or paprika

Directions:

1. Prepare the cucumber: Wash the cucumber and cut it into 1/2-inch thick slices.
2. Mix the cream cheese mixture: In a small bowl, combine the cream cheese, chopped dill, lemon zest, salt, and pepper. Mix until smooth and well combined.
3. Assemble the bites: Using a small spoon or a piping bag, dollop or pipe a generous amount of the cream cheese mixture onto each cucumber slice.
4. Add garnishes: If desired, top each cucumber bite with a small piece of smoked salmon, a sprig of dill, or a sprinkle of paprika for extra flavor and decoration.
5. Chill and serve: Refrigerate the cucumber and cream cheese bites for at least 30 minutes before serving to allow the flavors to meld and the cream cheese to firm up slightly.

Nutritional Values (per serving, about 3 bites):

- Calories: 50
- Fat: 4.5g
- Carbohydrates: 1g
- Protein: 1g

Roasted Veggie Chips

Ingredients:

- 1 sweet potato
- 1 beet
- 1 parsnip
- 1 carrot
- 2 tablespoons olive oil
- Salt to taste
- Optional seasonings: paprika, garlic powder, or rosemary

Directions:

1. Preheat the oven: Set your oven to 375°F (190°C). Line two baking sheets with parchment paper.
2. Prepare the vegetables: Wash and peel the sweet potato, beet, parsnip, and carrot. Using a mandoline slicer or a sharp knife, slice the vegetables into very thin rounds.
3. Season the veggies: In a large bowl, toss the sliced vegetables

with olive oil and salt. If desired, add any optional seasonings like paprika, garlic powder, or rosemary for additional flavor.
4. Arrange on baking sheets: Spread the vegetable slices in a single layer on the prepared baking sheets, making sure they don't overlap to ensure even cooking.
5. Bake: Place the baking sheets in the preheated oven and bake for 20-25 minutes, or until the veggie chips are crispy and lightly browned. It's important to watch them closely as they can easily burn. Rotate the pans and flip the chips halfway through cooking to ensure even crispiness.
6. Cool and serve: Remove the veggie chips from the oven and let them cool on the baking sheets for a few minutes; they will continue to crisp up as they cool. Serve immediately or store in an airtight container once fully cooled.

Nutritional Values (per serving, about a handful):

- Calories: 120
- Fat: 7g
- Carbohydrates: 13g
- Protein: 1g

Almond & Date Protein Bars

Ingredients:

- 1 cup pitted dates
- 1 cup raw almonds
- 1/4 cup protein powder (vanilla or unflavored)
- 1/4 cup unsweetened shredded coconut
- 2 tablespoons chia seeds
- 1 teaspoon vanilla extract
- 1/4 teaspoon salt

Directions:

1. Prepare the mixture: In a food processor, combine the pitted dates and almonds. Process until the mixture forms a coarse paste. Add the protein powder, shredded coconut, chia seeds, vanilla extract, and salt. Continue to process until all ingredients are well incorporated and the mixture sticks together when pressed between your fingers.
2. Form the bars: Line an 8x8 inch baking pan with parchment paper, allowing some overhang for easy removal. Transfer the mixture to the pan and press down firmly into an even layer. You can use the back of a spoon or the bottom of a measuring cup to help press the mixture flat.
3. Chill to set: Refrigerate the mixture for at least 2-3 hours, or until firm. This helps the bars to set and makes them easier to cut.
4. Cut into bars: Once chilled and firm, lift the mixture out of the pan using the overhanging parchment

paper. Place on a cutting board and slice into bars or squares.
5. Store: Keep the protein bars in an airtight container in the refrigerator for up to a week or freeze for longer storage.
6. Serve: Enjoy these Almond & Date Protein Bars as a nutritious snack, perfect for a post-workout recovery or a midday energy boost.

Nutritional Values (per bar, if cut into 12 bars):

- Calories: 150
- Fat: 8g
- Carbohydrates: 18g
- Protein: 5g

Sweet Potato Chips with Guacamole

Ingredients:

For the Sweet Potato Chips:

- 2 large sweet potatoes
- 2 tablespoons olive oil
- Salt to taste
- Optional: smoked paprika or ground cumin for extra flavor

For the Guacamole:

- 2 ripe avocados
- Juice of 1 lime
- 1/4 cup finely chopped red onion
- 1 small tomato, diced
- 1 clove garlic, minced
- Salt and pepper to taste
- Optional: chopped cilantro or a pinch of cayenne pepper for extra kick

Directions:

1. Preheat the oven: Set your oven to 375°F (190°C). Line a baking sheet with parchment paper.
2. Prepare the sweet potato chips: Wash and thinly slice the sweet potatoes using a mandoline slicer or a sharp knife for consistent thickness. Toss the sweet potato slices in olive oil and salt, and if using, add smoked paprika or ground cumin. Spread the slices in a single layer on the prepared baking sheet, ensuring they do not overlap.
3. Bake the sweet potato chips: Bake for about 20-25 minutes, or until crispy and slightly browned. Flip the chips halfway through to ensure even cooking. Keep a close eye on them to prevent burning.
4. Make the guacamole while the chips bake: In a medium bowl, mash the avocados with a fork. Stir in the lime juice, red onion, tomato, and garlic. Season with salt and pepper, and if desired, add cilantro or cayenne pepper. Mix well until combined.
5. Serve: Once the sweet potato chips are done, let them cool slightly to crisp up further. Serve immediately with the fresh guacamole for dipping.

Nutritional Values (per serving):

- Calories: 320
- Fat: 20g
- Carbohydrates: 35g
- Protein: 4g

Edamame Beans with Sea Salt

Ingredients:

- 2 cups frozen edamame beans (in their pods)
- 1 tablespoon olive oil or melted coconut oil
- 1-2 teaspoons sea salt, to taste

Directions:

1. Cook the edamame: Bring a pot of water to a boil. Add the frozen edamame beans and cook for about 5 minutes, or until they are fully heated through and tender.
2. Drain and season: Drain the edamame beans and toss them in a bowl with olive oil or melted coconut oil. Sprinkle sea salt over the beans, adjusting the amount according to your taste preferences.
3. Serve: Serve the edamame warm as a snack or appetizer. Encourage diners to pop the beans out of the pods directly into their mouths, discarding the pods.

Nutritional Values (per serving):

- Calories: 190
- Fat: 9g
- Carbohydrates: 13g
- Protein: 17g
- Fiber: 8g

Apple & Walnuts with Cinnamon

Ingredients:

- 2 medium apples, cored and chopped
- 1/2 cup walnuts, roughly chopped
- 1/2 teaspoon ground cinnamon
- Optional: a drizzle of honey or maple syrup for added sweetness

Directions:

1. Prepare the apples: Wash, core, and chop the apples into bite-sized pieces.
2. Mix ingredients: In a mixing bowl, combine the chopped apples, walnuts, and ground cinnamon. Toss everything together until the apples and walnuts are well-coated with cinnamon.
3. Add sweetness if desired: If you like a sweeter snack, drizzle a bit of honey or maple syrup over the mixture and toss again to evenly distribute the sweetness.
4. Serve: Enjoy this snack immediately, or let it sit for a few minutes to allow the flavors to meld together slightly.

Nutritional Values (per serving):

- Calories: 210
- Fat: 12g
- Carbohydrates: 25g

- Protein: 3g
- Fiber: 4g

Zucchini Fries with Avocado Dip

Ingredients:

For the Zucchini Fries:

- 4 medium zucchinis
- 1/2 cup all-purpose flour (or almond flour for a gluten-free option)
- 2 eggs, beaten
- 1 cup panko breadcrumbs (gluten-free breadcrumbs can be used)
- 1 teaspoon garlic powder
- 1 teaspoon paprika
- Salt and pepper to taste
- Cooking spray or oil

For the Avocado Dip:

- 1 ripe avocado
- Juice of 1 lime
- 1 clove garlic, minced
- 1/4 cup plain yogurt or sour cream
- Salt and pepper to taste
- Optional: cilantro or parsley for added flavor

Directions:

1. Preheat the oven: Set your oven to 425°F (220°C). Line a baking sheet with parchment paper and lightly grease it with cooking spray or a brush of oil.
2. Prepare the zucchini: Wash the zucchinis and cut them into fries-sized sticks. Pat dry with paper towels to remove excess moisture.
3. Dredge the zucchini fries: Set up three shallow bowls - one for flour, one for beaten eggs, and one for panko mixed with garlic powder, paprika, salt, and pepper. Dip each zucchini stick in flour, shake off excess, then dip in egg, and finally coat with the panko mixture. Place the coated zucchini fries on the prepared baking sheet.
4. Bake the zucchini fries: Bake in the preheated oven for about 20-25 minutes, turning halfway through, until golden and crispy.
5. Make the avocado dip: While the fries are baking, mash the avocado in a bowl. Mix in lime juice, minced garlic, yogurt or sour cream, and salt and pepper to taste. Stir in chopped cilantro or parsley if using.
6. Serve: Serve the baked zucchini fries hot with the creamy avocado dip on the side.

Nutritional Values (per serving):

- Calories: 290
- Fat: 15g
- Carbohydrates: 30g
- Protein: 10g

Chia Seed Crackers

Ingredients:

- 1/2 cup chia seeds
- 1/2 cup flax seeds

- 1/4 cup pumpkin seeds
- 1/4 cup sunflower seeds
- 1 cup water
- 1/2 teaspoon salt
- Optional seasonings: 1/2 teaspoon garlic powder, 1/2 teaspoon onion powder, or herbs like rosemary or thyme

Directions:

1. Preheat the oven: Set your oven to 325°F (163°C). Line a baking sheet with parchment paper.
2. Mix the ingredients: In a large bowl, combine chia seeds, flax seeds, pumpkin seeds, sunflower seeds, salt, and any optional seasonings. Add water and stir until everything is well mixed. Let the mixture sit for about 15-20 minutes, or until the chia and flax seeds have absorbed the water and the mixture becomes gelatinous.
3. Spread the mixture: Pour the seed mixture onto the prepared baking sheet. Using a spatula or the back of a spoon, spread the mixture evenly until it's about 1/8 inch thick. Try to make it as even as possible to ensure uniform cooking.
4. Bake the crackers: Place the baking sheet in the oven and bake for 30 minutes. Remove the baking sheet, cut the partially baked mixture into desired cracker shapes, then return to the oven and bake for another 30 minutes, or until completely dry and crisp. If needed, turn off the oven and let the crackers sit inside to dry out further without burning.
5. Cool and store: Allow the crackers to cool completely on the baking sheet. They will continue to crisp up as they cool. Once cool, store the chia seed crackers in an airtight container.

Nutritional Values (per serving, about 5 crackers):

- Calories: 150
- Fat: 9g
- Carbohydrates: 13g
- Protein: 6g
- Fiber: 9g

Cinnamon-Spiced Almonds

Ingredients:

- 2 cups whole almonds
- 1 tablespoon melted coconut oil or olive oil
- 2 tablespoons honey or maple syrup
- 1 teaspoon ground cinnamon
- 1/4 teaspoon salt
- Optional: pinch of nutmeg or ground cloves for extra spice

Directions:

1. Preheat the oven: Set your oven to 300°F (150°C). Line a baking sheet with parchment paper.

2. Prepare the almonds: In a large bowl, combine the almonds with melted coconut oil or olive oil, ensuring all the almonds are evenly coated.
3. Season the almonds: Add honey or maple syrup, ground cinnamon, salt, and any optional spices like nutmeg or cloves. Toss everything together until the almonds are evenly coated.
4. Bake the almonds: Spread the almonds in a single layer on the prepared baking sheet. Bake for 20-25 minutes, stirring occasionally, until the almonds are toasted and the coating is dry.
5. Cool and serve: Remove the almonds from the oven and allow them to cool completely on the baking sheet. They will become crunchier as they cool.
6. Store: Once cool, store the cinnamon-spiced almonds in an airtight container at room temperature.

Nutritional Values (per serving, about 1/4 cup):

- Calories: 220
- Fat: 18g
- Carbohydrates: 12g
- Protein: 6g
- Fiber: 4g

Coconut Yogurt with Berries

Ingredients:

- 1 cup coconut yogurt (plain or vanilla flavored)
- 1/2 cup mixed berries (such as blueberries, raspberries, and strawberries)
- 1 tablespoon honey or maple syrup (optional, for added sweetness)
- Optional toppings: a sprinkle of granola, chia seeds, or shredded coconut

Directions:

1. Prepare the berries: Wash the berries thoroughly. If using strawberries, hull and slice them into smaller pieces to match the size of the other berries.
2. Assemble the parfait: In a serving bowl or glass, spoon the coconut yogurt as the base layer. Top with the mixed berries, evenly distributing them over the yogurt.
3. Add sweetness and toppings: Drizzle honey or maple syrup over the berries if desired for extra sweetness. Sprinkle with optional toppings like granola, chia seeds, or shredded coconut for added texture and flavor.
4. Serve immediately: Enjoy this Coconut Yogurt with Berries as a refreshing and healthy snack or dessert, perfect for a quick breakfast or a mid-afternoon treat.

Nutritional Values (per serving):

- Calories: 180
- Fat: 9g
- Carbohydrates: 22g
- Protein: 5g

Grilled Veggie Skewers

Ingredients:

- 1 red bell pepper, cut into 1-inch pieces
- 1 yellow bell pepper, cut into 1-inch pieces
- 1 zucchini, sliced into 1/2-inch thick rounds
- 1 yellow squash, sliced into 1/2-inch thick rounds
- 1 red onion, cut into wedges
- 8-10 cherry tomatoes
- 2 tablespoons olive oil
- 1 teaspoon dried oregano
- 1 teaspoon garlic powder
- Salt and pepper to taste
- Optional: balsamic vinegar or lemon juice for drizzling

Directions:

- Preheat the grill: Preheat your grill to medium-high heat.
- Prepare the vegetables: In a large bowl, combine the bell peppers, zucchini, yellow squash, red onion, and cherry tomatoes. Drizzle with olive oil and sprinkle with oregano, garlic powder, salt, and pepper. Toss to coat evenly.
- Assemble the skewers: Thread the vegetables onto skewers, alternating between the different types to create a colorful arrangement.
- Grill the skewers: Place the skewers on the grill and cook for 10-15 minutes, turning occasionally, until the vegetables are tender and lightly charred.
- Finish and serve: If desired, drizzle balsamic vinegar or lemon juice over the grilled skewers for added flavor before serving.

Nutritional Values (per serving, assuming 4 servings):

- Calories: 120
- Fat: 7g
- Carbohydrates: 13g
- Protein: 2g

Chocolate-Covered Almonds

Ingredients:

- 1 cup raw almonds
- 1/2 cup dark chocolate chips (or dark chocolate bar, chopped)
- 1/2 teaspoon coconut oil (optional, for smoother chocolate)
- Pinch of sea salt (optional)

Directions:

1. Toast the almonds (optional): Preheat the oven to 350°F (175°C). Spread the almonds in a single layer on a baking sheet and toast for 8-10 minutes, stirring halfway

through. Allow them to cool completely before proceeding.
2. Melt the chocolate: In a microwave-safe bowl, combine the dark chocolate chips and coconut oil. Microwave in 20-second intervals, stirring in between, until the chocolate is completely melted and smooth. Alternatively, use a double boiler to melt the chocolate.
3. Coat the almonds: Add the almonds to the melted chocolate and stir until each almond is fully coated.
4. Arrange the almonds: Using a fork or slotted spoon, lift the chocolate-coated almonds out one by one, letting the excess chocolate drip off. Place them on a parchment-lined baking sheet in a single layer.
5. Sprinkle with sea salt (optional): While the chocolate is still wet, sprinkle a pinch of sea salt over the almonds for a sweet-and-salty flavor.
6. Chill to set: Place the baking sheet in the refrigerator for about 30 minutes, or until the chocolate is firm.
7. Store and serve: Transfer the chocolate-covered almonds to an airtight container and store in the refrigerator for up to 2 weeks. Enjoy as a sweet and satisfying snack!

Nutritional Values (per serving, about 1/4 cup):

- Calories: 180
- Fat: 12g
- Carbohydrates: 14g
- Protein: 4g

Cucumber & Hummus Bites

Ingredients:

- 1 large cucumber
- 1/2 cup hummus (flavor of your choice)
- Optional toppings: cherry tomatoes, sliced olives, red pepper flakes, or fresh parsley

Directions:

1. Prepare the cucumber: Wash the cucumber and slice it into 1/2-inch thick rounds. Arrange the slices on a serving plate.
2. Add the hummus: Using a spoon or a piping bag for a neater presentation, place a dollop of hummus on top of each cucumber slice.
3. Garnish: Top each bite with optional toppings like halved cherry tomatoes, sliced olives, a sprinkle of red pepper flakes, or a small sprig of parsley for added flavor and presentation.
4. Serve: Enjoy these cucumber and hummus bites immediately as a fresh, light snack or appetizer.

Nutritional Values (per serving, about 6 bites):

- Calories: 120
- Fat: 6g
- Carbohydrates: 10g
- Protein: 4g

Turmeric-Spiced Popcorn

Ingredients:

- 1/2 cup popcorn kernels
- 2 tablespoons coconut oil or olive oil
- 1 teaspoon ground turmeric
- 1/2 teaspoon paprika (optional)
- 1/2 teaspoon garlic powder
- Salt to taste

Directions:

1. Pop the kernels: Heat 1 tablespoon of the coconut or olive oil in a large pot over medium heat. Add the popcorn kernels and cover the pot with a lid. Shake the pot occasionally to ensure even popping. Continue until the popping slows down, then remove from heat.
2. Prepare the spice mix: In a small bowl, mix together the turmeric, paprika (if using), garlic powder, and salt.
3. Season the popcorn: Drizzle the remaining 1 tablespoon of oil over the warm popcorn, tossing to coat evenly. Sprinkle the spice mix over the popcorn and toss again until all the kernels are well-seasoned.
4. Serve: Enjoy immediately as a flavorful, healthy snack. Store any leftovers in an airtight container to keep fresh.

Nutritional Values (per serving, about 2 cups):

- Calories: 120
- Fat: 7g
- Carbohydrates: 12g
- Protein: 2g

CHAPTER 4

The 28-Day Meal Plan

Achieving long-term wellness doesn't have to be overwhelming. This 28-day meal plan is thoughtfully designed to guide you through a transformative journey toward balanced hormones, reduced stress, and sustainable weight management. By combining nutrient-rich meals with simple, achievable structure, this plan offers a practical way to nourish your body while supporting your overall health goals. Each day is carefully curated with recipes that prioritize whole foods and targeted ingredients to address hormonal imbalances and stress-related challenges. Whether you're looking to reset your routine or establish lasting habits, this roadmap is here to help you feel your best—one delicious meal at a time.

28 day meal plan chart

Days	Breakfast	Lunch	Dinner	Snack
1	Cinnamon Almond Oatmeal	Quinoa & Chickpea Salad with Lemon Tahini Dressing	Grilled Salmon with Roasted Brussels Sprouts and Quinoa	Avocado & Hummus Toast
2	Avocado & Spinach Smoothie	Grilled Chicken with Sweet Potato and Greens	Turmeric and Ginger Chicken Stir-Fry	Greek Yogurt & Berry Parfait
3	Turmeric Coconut	Avocado, Cucumber,	Spaghetti Squash	Protein-Packed

	Porridge	and Tomato Salad with Olive Oil Dressing	with Pesto and Grilled Chicken	Energy Balls
4	Chia Pudding with Berries	Turmeric Chicken Soup	Lemon & Herb Baked Cod with Steamed Vegetables	Carrot Sticks with Almond Butter
5	Egg White & Veggie Scramble	Lentil & Kale Soup	Zucchini Noodles with Avocado Pesto	Chocolate-Covered Almonds
6	Almond Flour Pancakes	Chia and Walnut Salad with Avocado and Lemon Vinaigrette	Grilled Chicken with Asparagus and Sweet Potato	Baked Sweet Potato Fries
7	Protein-Packed Smoothie	Salmon Salad with Spinach and Walnuts	Cauliflower & Chickpea Curry	Cucumber & Cream Cheese Bites
8	Sweet Potato Hash with Poached Eggs	Miso Soup with Tofu and Seaweed	Grilled Tempeh with Brussels Sprouts	Apple with Almond Butter & Cinnamon
9	Flaxseed & Banana Muffins	Eggplant & Lentil Stew	Grilled Chicken Caesar Salad with Greek Yogurt Dressing	Spicy Roasted Pumpkin Seeds
10	Zucchini & Mushroom Frittata	Salmon & Broccoli Stir-Fry	Sweet Potato & Black Bean Chili	Greek Yogurt & Berry Parfait
11	Matcha & Almond Butter Smoothie	Quinoa & Black Bean Buddha Bowl	Coconut & Lime Chicken with Mango Salad	Protein-Packed Energy Balls
12	Overnight Oats with Walnuts and Berries	Turkey & Avocado Lettuce Wraps	Spicy Quinoa & Vegetable Stir-Fry	Baked Sweet Potato Fries
13	Coconut & Chia Seed Pudding	Grilled Veggie & Halloumi Salad	Lemon Garlic Chicken with Sautéed Spinach	Chocolate-Covered Almonds
14	Avocado Toast with Lemon and Pumpkin Seeds	Asian-Inspired Salmon Salad	Cauliflower Rice Stir-Fry with Vegetables	Carrot Sticks with Almond Butter
15	Apple Cinnamon Quinoa	Grilled Tofu with Spinach & Pine Nuts	Garlic Butter Shrimp with	Greek Yogurt & Berry Parfait

				Zoodles
16	Kefir & Berry Parfait	Chickpea & Sweet Potato Buddha Bowl	Baked Salmon with Broccoli and Lemon	Spicy Roasted Pumpkin Seeds
17	Carrot Cake Oats	Cabbage & Carrot Slaw with Avocado	Spaghetti Squash Primavera	Protein-Packed Energy Balls
18	Coconut Milk Chia Pudding	Grilled Chicken with Mango Salsa and Brown Rice	Coconut-Lime Grilled Fish Tacos	Baked Sweet Potato Fries
19	Egg & Avocado Breakfast Wrap	Baked Salmon with Broccoli and Lemon	Spicy Turkey Meatballs with Cauliflower Rice	Greek Yogurt & Berry Parfait
20	Berry & Hemp Protein Smoothie	Miso-Glazed Salmon with Cucumber Salad	Eggplant & Lentil Stew with Garlic Bread	Spicy Roasted Pumpkin Seeds
21	Cinnamon-Spiced Quinoa Porridge	Grilled Chicken with Roasted Vegetables	Sweet Potato & Black Bean Tacos	Greek Yogurt & Berry Parfait
22	Green Detox Smoothie	Lemon Herb Chicken with Roasted Sweet Potatoes	Teriyaki Salmon with Veggie Stir-Fry	Chocolate-Covered Almonds
23	Pumpkin Spice Chia Pudding	Sweet Potato & Kale Buddha Bowl	Grilled Steak with Roasted Vegetables	Protein-Packed Energy Balls
24	Peanut Butter & Banana Oats	Roasted Veggie & Quinoa Stir-Fry	Salmon & Avocado Wraps	Baked Sweet Potato Fries
25	Mango Coconut Smoothie	Grilled Veggie Skewers	Lemon Garlic Chicken with Sautéed Spinach	Greek Yogurt & Berry Parfait
26	Cinnamon Almond Oatmeal	Spaghetti Squash with Pesto and Grilled Chicken	Zucchini Noodles with Avocado Pesto	Chocolate-Covered Almonds
27	Avocado & Spinach Smoothie	Turmeric Chicken Soup	Grilled Chicken with Asparagus and	Carrot Sticks with Almond

			Sweet Potato	Butter
28	Turmeric Coconut Porridge	Avocado, Cucumber, and Tomato Salad with Olive Oil Dressing	Cauliflower & Chickpea Curry	Greek Yogurt & Berry Parfait

Made in United States
North Haven, CT
05 July 2025